HOOKED
ON
LIFE

HOOKED
ON
LIFE

How to Totally Recover from Addictions & Codependency

Tim Timmons
and
Stephen Arterburn

A Division of Thomas Nelson Publishers
Nashville

Published in Nashville, Tennessee, by Oliver-Nelson Books, a division of Thomas Nelson, Inc., Publishers, and distributed in Canada by Lawson Falle, Ltd., Cambridge, Ontario.

Unless specifically identified as factual, all names and events have been fictionalized for protection of privacy.

Printed in the United States of America.

ISBN 0-8407-9562-9

Library of Congress Cataloging-in-Publication Data

Timmons, Tim.
  Hooked on life : how to totally recover from addictions & codependency / Tim Timmons and Stephen Arterburn.
      p. cm.
  ISBN 0-8407-9562-9
  1. Compulsive behavior. 2. Co-dependency. I. Arterburn, Stephen, 1953-   . II. Title.
RC533.T56 1989
616.86—dc19

                                                        88-38480
                                                          CIP

Dedication

To all who have become the victims
of addiction and codependency.

May this book be the beginning of a
never-ending process of recovery.

Victims no more!

Contents

Acknowledgments

Our deepest and most sincere appreciation goes to Victor Oliver and Lila Empson. Their contributions and guidance made this book significantly stronger.

Introduction

Two universal things are common to all human beings: (1) people develop addictions, and (2) those close to the addicts become codependent on the addict and the addiction. But no matter how deep we go into addiction and codependency, we can start over, we can recover. There is hope, no matter how stuck we become in addiction or codependency.

Hooked on Life is for everyone who hurts. It doesn't demand dramatic or miraculous choices and changes. It requires making only one decision at a time and living only one day at a time.

Hooked on Life's principles will help you and your family move out of addiction and codependency. It will help you get unstuck and guide you through the process of starting over. It will lead you from lonely struggling with your problems to sharing your solutions. It is a step into recovery.

Recovery involves a series of choices and a sensible change in your lifestyle.

You will be at the starting point of renewed health and happiness. Every area of your life—psychological, social, physical, mental, and spiritual—will come into balance as you discover who you are, what you are doing, and where you are going.

Getting *Hooked on Life* can be the most exciting adventure of your life!

Stuck:
No One Is Exempt

stuck, *v.* to be brought to a standstill, blocked, baffled, halted, obstructed; *n.* a state of difficulty or hesitation.

Some People Who Got Stuck

Everybody's stuck sometime, addicted, dependent, or co-dependent on someone who is. Let's look at a few examples of people who got stuck in their lives. These testimonies are the words of actual people with only names and a few minor facts changed to preserve anonymity.

University Student: Majors in More than Economics

"I knew I had a problem with drugs and alcohol in high school when I was fifteen years old. Many days at lunch time I'd go behind the school and get drunk. Then I would miss the rest of my classes during the day. Eventually I began drinking before and after school as well as at lunch time. It just kept progressing week by week. One day I got tired of the alcohol and turned on to pot, just to get rid of the pain in my life. It seemed to be the only way that I could feel comfortable.

"The worst time of my drinking and drug addiction was when I was twenty years old. It had gotten so bad. I was getting high, drinking as much as possible, using any kind of drugs that were available as many times as I could a day. One night I

realized I would never be able to live my life without being dependent on chemicals. I'd given up hope of being free. I was miserable. I tried to end my life one night in my car."
Stuck: *Alcohol. Drugs.*

Business Executive: Manages Everything but His Own Life

"My business was going great! I was making all the money I ever imagined that I ever wanted to make, but the other parts of my life weren't going well. I had a hard time relating to people. I had failed in two marriages and hadn't been a good father. I spent a lot of hours on the job—close to a hundred hours a week. People kept telling me to delegate and turn things over to others. But I thought it was easier to do it myself than to go around and check up on somebody else later.

"I was pretty despondent about breaking up with my second wife. We lived together for two years after we were divorced, and then we broke up all over again. I was desperate to put my life back together."
Stuck: *Workaholism.*

"Teen-Age" Woman: Hits Puberty at 33

"I ended up a lot of times in jail and a couple of times in a mental hospital. That really upset me—especially when I woke up with all those psychos around—because I've always been independent and have done what I wanted to do. I didn't know how to take anyone's advice, or even want to. When I ended up in the jail and heard those doors clang shut, I knew I couldn't get out. I also knew I wasn't going anyplace in my life. I couldn't get out and the people who kept the keys had me at their mercy.

"At my worst moments, locked in a cell, I'd have nothing to do but think. During those times I had all kinds of pain—psychic, mental, and spiritual—and all of it inside. But once I got on the outside, I'd do something crazy or freak out and the next thing I knew, they'd lock me up again. But I couldn't seem to stop doing those things. I even tried to kill myself three times. The first time I cut my wrists. Then I started burning myself with matches all over my body. I kept doing crazy things like that because I wanted it to show on the outside, on my body, the way the pain was killing me on the inside. And, you know, it kind of helped. And in some kind of crazy way, it calmed me down.

"I got into booze, drugs, and all kinds of rebellion. I guess that's when I lost any kind of conscience until I didn't even know anymore when I did right and when I did wrong. Now I'm trying to grow up all over again. *Puberty hits hard at thirty-three.* It's not easy when I suddenly find myself only thirteen years old emotionally and having to repeat all my stages of growth."
Stuck: *Alcohol. Drugs. Suicide. Rebellion.*

Songwriter: Singing in the Pain

"At the top of my career, I had already won two Academy Awards for the best song and five Golden Globes. But inside, I was a desperately unhappy man. It sounds strange to talk about being unhappy when I had achieved so much in my field, but I had never learned to live with myself. I was what some call an overachiever, and others call a workaholic. In order to keep going and work under the pressures, I got heavily into Valium. Then when I gained so much weight, I took uppers to lose. It got so bad that I felt trapped in my own home, and I became what I later learned is an agoraphobic. An agoraphobic is a person who fears open places.

"On top of all that, my wife and I separated for three weeks. During that period, my dad died without having ever told me that he loved me. I was a driven man, and I was driving myself to destruction. Worst of all, I didn't know where to turn for help. A lot of my friends were worse off than me."
Stuck: *Workaholism. Phobias. Drugs. Relationships.*

Another University Student: Loves a Liquid Lunch

"I knew I had a problem at fifteen because every day at school lunch break my friends and I drank liquid lunches. We'd sneak beer from home, drink during school, and then go to classes wasted. When I went away to college, I started writing bad checks and using cocaine. I kept lying to myself, 'It's only going to be this once and then I'm going to quit.' But I didn't quit. My habit got so bad I stole everything I could get my hands on and converted it to cash.

"The worst time for me came when they put me in jail for DUI [driving under the influence]. I had to spend the whole night there. Sitting in that cell all night thinking of what a mess I'd made of everything, that's when I knew I had to do something or get some help. For the first time since I was fourteen, I wanted to do something—anything—to solve my problem."
Stuck: *Alcohol. Drugs.*

Nurse: Molested by "Loving" Father

"I didn't know how to maintain any kind of relationship. Both of my marriages to alcoholics ended in divorce. In addition to my two alcoholic husbands, I had one other long-term relationship. He was also an alcoholic, but I stayed with him longer than I had with anyone else. But that ended in catastrophe, like all the others. Even everyday relationships with people at work were bad. I always resisted authority with anger and resentment. I never allowed anyone into my life, never let anyone get close enough to love me. I never felt I deserved anyone's love. I didn't have a lot of love to give either, I suppose. I was just not much of a human being. I only wanted to keep everyone at a distance—even my own son.

"I have a nineteen-year-old son. I know I've never loved him the way he wanted to be loved, and I never let him love me, either. Steve always wanted a father—a real father, not a temporary one. He wanted a man in his life he could respect. He saw the parade of men, and he also saw tragedy after tragedy because none of the relationships lasted. Steve and I developed a terrible relationship, or maybe I ought to say, no relationship. He was angry with me, and several times he even threatened to kill me with his fists. One time he threatened me with a gun. He hated me for all the rotten things that had happened in his life.

"During all this time of fighting with Steve, I ate. I ate constantly, isolating myself and staying away from people. I hid in the house, not wanting to go anywhere except to work. When I came home from work every day, I'd start to nibble on something and would keep on eating until I fell asleep at night. When I got off work on Fridays, I ate almost without stopping until I went back to work on Monday. That constant food abuse went on for two years. Then I hit bottom.

"All those years anger had been driving me into alcohol, drugs, food, and work. Instead of helping, the anger only seemed to get worse. Then one day someone said, 'You are so angry. Why are you angry all the time?' I blurted out the answer. For the first time I said the words out loud: 'Because my father molested me!' All my life I had lived as though I loved and idolized my father.

"But I can't cover it up any more. He began to molest me when I was thirteen, and he kept doing it until I left for college five years later. He destroyed my whole childhood. Not only did my father betray me, but so did my mother. She knew what he was doing but wouldn't ever say or do anything about it. Both of them betrayed me, and I'm still angry. Now I can't face my parents, even thirty years later, because of what happened in my childhood."

Stuck: *Relationships. Parenting. Alcohol. Drugs. Food. Molestation.*

Homemaker: Loses 15, Gains 20

"I am a blob. I'm five feet two and weigh 320 pounds. I've been on every diet I've ever heard of. Over the years I've lost weight hundreds of times, but I gain it all back each time—and add a few more pounds—as soon as I stop the diet. I feel hopeless. I lose fifteen pounds and I gain back twenty."

Stuck: *Food.*

Secretary: Living with a Dead Daughter

"Last year the police came to my door and announced that my daughter overdosed on drugs. Dead. Gone. I couldn't believe it. A hundred times I've told myself that I shouldn't have let her go out with that crowd. She was only sixteen. She didn't

even know what she was doing. But I let her go with them. How can I ever live with myself?"
Stuck: *Death. Guilt.*

Cheerleader: Lost Her Cheerfulness and Her Leg

"My mother always warned me never to ride a motorcycle. But when Billy asked me to hop on the back, it seemed harmless. We took off so fast. It was so much fun, and then the worst thing possible happened—we skidded head-on into a tractor-trailer. Billy tried to get out of the way, but we had no chance. When it was all over, my right leg was gone. Why me? One time ever on a motorcycle, and then handicapped for life. No more normal anything for me. I'm through with people, school, and life. Who wants a handicapped cheerleader?"
Stuck: *Handicap.*

Some of these illustrations may sound a little extreme—and they are. People have an unbelievable ability to take problems, compound them to the limits, and still manage to live through them. We all get stuck at times. Here's one example of how and when I got stuck:

I became drunk with credit. Just out of college and with a new job, I obtained access to thousands of dollars worth of credit within a few weeks. I filled out every application I ran across, and the cards came rolling in. It was amazing. I bought a $500 television set and only had to pay $20 a month for the pleasure of fine viewing. To further add to my enjoyment, I found that I could buy a $100 sofa on which to sit while viewing the $500 TV set and only have to pay $15 a month for the comfort. To further enhance my pleasure, I completely recarpeted the house for $3,000 and only had to pay $40 a month for the new floor on which to set my TV and sofa. And that was only the beginning. By the time I was finished, I had used the maximum credit available on all the accounts, and I didn't have enough money to make even the minimum payments.

What I needed, I thought, was just one more credit card to cover the monthly minimums of the other cards. It was a mess, and I was definitely messed up. Stuck is a more appropriate term. Stores, collection agencies, and credit card companies tugged, nagged, and demanded money immediately. Fortunately, a credit counseling agency helped me to get unstuck and start over. It was hard admitting that I could not handle the problem alone, but it was a relief to be able to start over.

Stuck Comes in All Varieties

As these stories illustrate, stuck shows itself in a lot of different forms: alcohol, drugs, workaholism, food, disease, suicide, death, molestation, divorce, relationships, rebellion, anger, guilt, phobias, handicaps, loneliness.

When we examine them, some forms of stuck—such as alcohol and drug abuse—seem worse and have a greater stigma. Others—such as death, deadly disease, and physical handicaps—seem to be victimizing attacks against humanity. Less obvious are the more common forms of stuck—such as compulsive work, hidden spouse or child abuse, divorce for convenience, impulsive affairs, disguised loneliness, occasional or chain smoking. We rarely mark these situations as desperate problems. But they are. And you can get stuck in them.

We overlook and underrate problems like these for two reasons. First, we look at our own problems and think "They're not so bad. I can handle them on my own." From our own perspective, we deny the problems and reject their magnitude. This denial is damaging. *Instead of people having the problems, the problems have the people.*

Second, we look at other people's problems and *still* think of our own, "Your problems aren't as bad as mine." When problems belong to others, they're just another set of problems. But they become difficult crises when they happen to us! In reality, we all have serious problems at one time or another; yet in our society, we deny the desperation in each other. *Until we face our desperation honestly, we won't get any better.* That's the first tenet of getting hooked on life.

We Are All Stuck

That's right—*all* of us, and no exceptions. It doesn't matter where we look, whether we turn to our doctors, our neighbors, our ministers, our friends, or even our counselors, all of us (at least at one time or another) are stuck.

Strange, isn't it, that our enlightened society knows more and can do more than at any other time in world history, yet stuck is still around. We have more self-help information and programs than ever before in virtually every known problem area. Yet stuck is not only around, it keeps growing. Think about it. The divorce rate remains at an intolerable level. Drug and food abuse are on the increase. Alcoholism negatively affects one-third of all American families. A recent study on molestation predicts that 28 per cent of girls will have been molested by the time they reach fourteen, and by the age of eighteen, that figure goes up to 38 per cent.[1] We may know more *about* life, but we still don't know how to *live* life.

If we remain stuck, we go nowhere, we do little that promotes life, and we view life from a narrow perspective. Being stuck is like hanging by a skyhook. The hook controls us, and we can't enjoy stability or make progress. Life demands growth (stability and progress), but stuck stunts human growth. Stuck drains our lives and drives us toward self-destruction.

We are all stuck. Sound depressing? The good news is that we can start over. We can recover.

We Can All Start Over

We can get *Hooked on Life* and go from stuck to starting over! That's exciting news, because as human beings we have two universal things in common: (1) we are all stuck; and (2) we can all start over. No matter how we got stuck, we can apply certain proven principles that enable us to start over.

Starting over involves a series of choices and a sensible change in our lifestyles. *Hooked on Life* doesn't demand dra-

---

1. *USA Today*, August 7, 1984.

matic or miraculous choices and changes. *Hooked on Life* requires only that we make one decision at a time, that we learn to live one day at a time. *Hooked on Life* can help all of us recognize the paralysis that makes us stuck, and we can learn how to respond to the principles of starting over.

Getting Stuck
in Life's Pressures

A truck driver was making his way across town faithfully following the designated route. But something was strange about this driver. Every time he came to a stop light or stop sign, he jumped out and repeatedly beat the truck with a huge baseball bat.

A curious observer followed this unusual driver until he maneuvered his truck into a restaurant parking lot. As soon as the truck stopped, the driver again jumped out and proceeded to beat the truck all the way around. The observer asked the obvious question, "Why do you beat your truck with a bat every time you stop?"

The driver said, "Well, it's like this. I have a two-ton truck and four tons of canaries, and I have to keep two tons in the air all the time!"

Four Tons of Canaries in a Two-Ton Truck

A lot of us are going through life with an extra ton or two of canaries. And every canary represents one more pressure that can set us up to get stuck and stay stuck. We need to get rid of the canaries that weight us down and keep us frustrated.

The canaries in our life—the pressures and stresses—are deceptive. Their presence can elude us for quite some time, but

28

they are always there. These pressures of life appear harmless, but they are like time bombs, ticking away, scheduled to blow up at some unknown time. These time bombs are an integral part of the modern-day existence that promotes our stuckness. The key is to identify and defuse these time bombs by developing an awareness of their effects. Futurists warn us of the time bombs still to come. Pessimists see them everywhere. Optimists deny them. But all of us must deal with them. Let's look at seven of the most destructive time bombs that work together to get us stuck and delay our fight to get unstuck.

1. The Ecological Time Bomb: Surviving the Crowd

You might ask, "What does ecology have to do with getting stuck?" Well, more than four billion people are in the world today. That's a lot of folks living on one small planet. The astounding thing is that the population is scheduled to double in fewer than forty years.[1] It's getting crowded. And the demand for food, housing, jobs, land, fresh water, and energy is increasing daily. The demand is growing, and the supply is shrinking. More than ten thousand people starve to death every day.[2]

As the environment changes in response to vast hordes of people inhabiting the earth and depleting its resources, a personal reaction is triggered. This reaction is an emotional stress pressing at the heart of each one of us. The tendency is to ignore feelings of despair at the uncontrollable population explosion. In the midst of the crowd, we tend to retreat into our own comfortable obsessions and compulsions as a means of survival. We struggle to cope and survive rather than to carry out plans for successful living. The world around us is changing so rapidly that if we do not adapt to the emotional pressures of a strained environment, we get stuck in our struggle to endure.

<hr />

1. "Population and the Sierra Club," San Francisco Sierra Club Newsletter, June 1975, p. 4.
2. Paul R. Erlich, *The Population Bomb* (New York: Ballantine Books, 1968), pp. 25, 26.

2. The Chemical Time Bomb: You Are What You Eat
. . . and Drink . . . and Drug

Researchers spend millions of dollars every year to determine which chemicals in our food and drinks may cause cancer, allergic reactions, headaches, and even death. The evidence is confusing and indecisive. For instance, vitamin C is said to prevent the common cold. But if it is left in the mouth too long, the same vitamin C can cause oral cancer.

Some Canadians published a study that labeled saccharin as a cancer-causing substance in rats. Shortly afterward, saccharin was banned in the USA.[3] A later study revealed that an individual would have to consume eight hundred twelve-ounce cans of Tab a day for a lifetime in order to ingest the same amount of saccharin that produced the cancer in the rats.[4] Saccharin was then allowed again. So which study is the most credible or believable?

But vitamin C and saccharin are mere firecrackers compared to the chemical time bombs ticking away in thousands of lives. The most destructive chemical time bombs are alcohol and drugs. The damage caused from the abuse of these chemicals is well documented:

- Every fifteen seconds a traffic accident occurs that involves both a teen-ager and alcohol.
- Every twenty-three minutes a teen-ager dies in an alcohol-related traffic accident.
- While the death rate is going down for adults, it is going up for teen-agers because of alcohol and traffic deaths.
- When alcohol, a teen-ager, and an automobile are mixed together, another time bomb awaits a deadly explosion.

The cost of drug abuse to the United States rose 286 per cent from 1977 to 1984. The cost increased from $16.4 billion to a whopping $46.9 billion. At the same time, the cost of alcoholism rose from $49.4 billion to $89.5 billion.[5] Whether it's

---

3. "FDA Bans Saccharin, Says It Causes Cancer in Animals," *Los Angeles Times*, 10 March 1977.
4. "The Ban on Saccharin: How? Why?" *Los Angeles Times*, 20 March 1977.
5. "Economic Cost to Society of Alcohol and Drug Abuse and Mental Illness," Research Triangle Institute, June 1984.

white mounds of cocaine or brownish-green bales of marijuana, chemical time bombs in this country are detonated daily. These bombs, more than any others, are exploding jobs, marriages, financial security, families, and lives. Cancer in Canadian rats pales to insignificance when compared to addiction in American people.

3. The Psychological Time Bomb: Weathering the Emotional Storms

Psychological time bombs can cripple our entire lifestyle because of their great influence on society. Most people have made little progress toward emotional stability and successful living. According to the National Institute of Mental Health:[6]
- 20 per cent of all Americans suffer from some type of mental illness within any given six-month period.
- Over thirteen million Americans suffer from anxiety or a phobia, and over nine million suffer from depression.
- Only one person in five who need help is receiving treatment for mental illness.

The suicide rate has never been higher. To the horror of Clear Lake High School in Texas, 1984 will be remembered as the year when six students committed suicide within two months. Since psychological experts differ so much in their opinions on how to maintain mental health, it is important that each individual has a system of values upon which to base decisions and develop emotional maturity.

Depression in America is almost epidemic. Paranoiacs can be found everywhere. And conflicting psychological theories produce confusion on how to live, how to raise children, and how to resolve problems. The results of these psychological time bombs are emotional turmoil and self-destruction. Unless they are defused, the agony and despair are endless.

4. The Biological Time Bomb: It's All in Your Genes

The cradle of life and the grave of death have long been matters confined to the discussion of philosophers and the descrip-

---

6. As reported from *USA Today*, 3 October 1984.

tion of poets. The first breath and the last were dictated by the supreme reign of nature, and each person lived and died under its rule. But now evidence from research and experience underscores the influence of biological predisposition on the development of human problems. These biological time bombs, however, can be identified and defused through complete lifestyle changes.

All of the evidence is not in yet pertaining to biological predisposition and heredity as they relate to problems. But some facts have become known. Biological predisposition, for example, has an extremely important impact on the development of coronary heart disease. A man whose father died of heart disease at age fifty-one must consider himself a high risk for a heart attack. For many, the heart is a time bomb that ticks toward death. But it is also known that diet, activity, exercise, and attitudinal changes can be made to counteract the biological influence on the heart's function and dysfunction.

Biological time bombs influence the future in many other areas. Studies show that 50 per cent of all alcoholics come from alcoholic homes. At first this might appear to be a sociological or psychological phenomenon. But consider some of the findings. The Goodwin studies out of Denmark[7] reveal a biological link for alcoholism. When identical twins of alcoholic parents were adopted into homes that were later classified as alcoholic and nonalcoholic, it was found that it made no difference whether or not the adoptive parents had a problem with alcohol—the alcoholism rate for the children was the same. But when adopted children whose natural parents were alcoholic were compared to adopted children whose natural parents were not alcoholic, it was discovered that the adopted children of alcoholic parents had six times the rate of alcoholism than that of adopted children born of nonalcoholic parents. Children of alcoholics need to be aware of the significance of their biological predisposition to alcohol problems. Their drinking can lead to a fast route toward alcoholism.

Many more biological time bombs produce problems for thousands of people. Whether it's cancer, diabetes, pre-

---

7. P. W. Goodwin, "Is Alcoholism Hereditary?" *Archives of General Psychiatry* 25:545-549.

menstrual syndrome, headaches, or heart disease, we must be able to accept these time bombs as reality, deal with them, and defuse them if we are to experience a successful lifestyle.

5. The Religious Time Bomb: Confusionism— Religion of the Masses

Religious time bombs comprise a mixed bag of tricks. It is no wonder confusion reigns throughout the world about God. God is presented with diverse and contradictory teachings. God is packaged as Thetan, Perfect Knowledge, Wholly Other, Krishna, or Jesus. God is offered under the auspices of *missions*, such as Scientology and Divine Light; of *mystics*, such as Krishna consciousness and Zen; of *families*, such as Children of God and Love Israel; of *churches*, such as Local and Unification; and of humanly devised religious *systems*, such as Catholic, Protestant, and Jewish. They all promise spiritual awareness leading to a more fruitful, happy life, a blissed-out existence of perfect peace, the way to God, or at least a "ticket" to heaven.

Conflicting ideas about who God is and what religion consists of lead to getting ourselves stuck. And none of us is alone in confusion. We see religious fanatics, bizarre cultists, and caricatures of godly people on television and throughout the community. Rather than encourage us to explore and discover the true nature of God, these extremists confuse us and push us away from God and spiritual growth. As a result, we set ourselves up as the highest source of power from which we can derive strength. Eventually, through years of emptiness and despair, religious time bombs produce self-destruction, narcissism, or an awareness that God is a real and dynamic part of our lives. The search for the nature of God and spiritual growth is the only means by which religious time bombs can be defused.

6. The Sociological Time Bomb: War on the Home Front

Sociological time bombs can be heard ticking away in the unresolved conflicts at every level of society. Among nations, the twentieth century has given us more wars than all of the previous centuries put together. The situation is illustrated by two

American Indians, stuck in a foxhole during a World War II air raid. "The way I figure it," one said, "is that when they smoked the peace pipe in 1918, nobody inhaled." Whether between nations, minorities, neighbors, or families, painful relationships are racked with conflict.

In our world of sociological sabotage, more and more relationships have been breaking up and falling into the witches' cauldron of toils and troubles. Sociologists tell us that the most dangerous place to be on a Friday night is not on the street but in many homes across the land. Family violence today is occurring in epidemic proportions. Among families, marriages are not working, parenting is less effective, and individuals are obsessed with self-satisfaction. Sociological time bombs are exploding in our homes.

Relationships of all types are filled with turmoil. Many simply are not working. As a result, people are abandoning the relationships and merely playing out roles in which only the most surface interaction is appropriate. It's the empty "Hi-how-are-you?" routine. A flood of empty words characterizes our shallow interactions with each other. The element of accountability between two people has been abandoned.

When there is no accountability, marriages become little more than live-in arrangements where personal intimacy is a fake. In addition, other relationships are maintained at an artificial, unfulfilling level. Women are alienated from other women. Men are hard-pressed to name one true friendship in which openness and honesty are key ingredients. Our society is a group of people in conflict, and that conflict is raging within the home. We trade true relationships and personal involvement for an alienated existence. We construct shells to hide the real person within.

7. The Philosophical Time Bomb: The Crisis of Rights and Wrongs

Philosophical time bombs leave society foundationless. A great corollary says, "If you've got one watch, you know what time it is. But if you've got two, you're never sure!"

We have lost the standards and values upon which we can

build meaningful existence. Instead, we rationalize what we do in three deteriorating stages: First, rather than be able to take a stand on the rightness or the wrongness of an action, we resort to, "It all depends on how you look at it." Next, that line of thinking gives way to, "You know, I've been thinking it over, and it really doesn't make any difference how you look at it." Finally, the rationalization is made, "I don't think *anyone* knows how to look at it!"

This is an age of some tough decisions. We are at an unprecedented point in history where our values will decide the fate of millions of lives. We must answer some difficult questions: Who should control life? Who should control death? *Should* we control life and death? Bold control of life and death uses such techniques as *genetic engineering* (creating and manipulating human life physically, mentally, and emotionally, according to design specifications) and *abortion* (extinguishing human life after conception but before natural birth). Control over who should live or die—and what kind of people will be born in the future—is an unresolved issue for us as a society and as individuals. If we have no foundation of values, we cannot build an ethical standard. It is no wonder that so much guilt and anxiety surround our decisions. Rather than resolving these issues by going with the flow or just doing what feels good, we need to return to a reliable system of standards in discerning right from wrong. When traditional values fall apart, the society crumbles from a faulty foundation.

Living with Emotions That Can Kill You

As the time bombs are planted and explode all around us, the three paralyses of fear, anger, and guilt form a deadly triad of disintegration. This triad of emotions sets us up for some devastating debris!

Paralysis One: Fear of Moving Forward

The enormity of seemingly insurmountable problems from all of our time bombs inflicts additional pressures on us, and we are faced with many unresolved emotions. As awareness of the magnitude of our problems increases, fear sets in. We become afraid of the unknown, afraid of the future that lies ahead. As our time bombs continue exploding in towering clouds of smoke, we fear that our future is out of control, that we can do nothing. Consequently if we act, we act aimlessly. It is as if we shoot arrows with no target in sight.

In fear, we lose our freedom to live comfortably and productively. And we create a false image to cover up for our fear. In fear, we lose faith. For people without a strong faith in self, in others, and in God, the fear becomes paralyzing. In fear, we get stuck. Rather than act and be found inadequate, we do nothing but maintain, survive, or hold on. That is not living, that is staying stuck.

Harry G. Mendelson said, "Courage is nothing but being equal to the problems and challenges before us." Time bombs give us a sense of inadequacy in the face of a complex and problem-filled world. The fact is, alone, we are inadequate. The most important step in overcoming inadequacy and fear is reaching out to one another in the struggle. An outstretched hand and a request for help are important first steps in moving from stuck to starting over. Together we become equal to the problems and challenges before us. Together we can get unstuck.

Paralysis Two: Anger That Festers

All of the time bombs that affect our relationships and our expectations result in anger. If we are out of control, we cannot fulfill one another's expectations, and we become angry. When we are teeming with unmet expectations, we become angry with others, with ourselves, with God, and with the world in general. This anger works to fortify our alienation and keep us stuck with destructive feelings. The angrier we become, the more we try to control people, circumstances, and all the other things that are uncontrollable. In our anger, we lose control of ourselves and the world around us.

Anger is expressed in a variety of ways, but its expression falls into two classifications. The first classification is *overt* (observable) anger. Hostility, rage, temper tantrums, murder, and self-destruction are forms of overt anger. The second classification is *covert* (concealed) anger. Depression is often called a temper tantrum turned inward. Suspicion, bereavement, teasing, and certain kinds of humor can all be the outward appearance of unresolved and suppressed anger.

The most common, and perhaps the most malignant, form of anger is resentment. Anger by itself is not destructive. We can channel this valid feeling into appropriate action and resolution. But when anger is allowed to fester, the residue of resentment eventually hardens into an all-consuming bitterness. Rather than endure the pain of verbally expressing angry feelings as they occur, most of us choose the repressive route. We become pros at throwing our angry thoughts and feelings down into the subconscious. We develop a pressure-cooker lifestyle, a lifestyle boiling with resentment and capable of blowing up at any time. We become apathetic because we are afraid that if someone gets to know us intimately, the cover will be blown and the pot of destructive anger discovered. Rather than shoot randomly without a target, as in the case of fear, we wonder why we should shoot at all. In fear of losing control, we avoid encounters that could add to the anger and put us over the brink into a world of total lack of control and unrelenting pain. When the pain becomes too great and care from others becomes too little, we ask, "Why relate at all? Why build more expectations that will go unmet?" These questions are the questions of a stuck person who needs to start over.

Paralysis Three: Guilt That Won't Forgive

Guilt is easily the major cause of human breakdown, and the feelings of guilt can cause a person to self-destruct faster than almost anything else. That's the nature of guilt—it seeks to punish us for our wrongdoings. The origin of guilt lies in the philosophical time bomb.[8] Some of us think we don't have a problem with guilt because we have everything well in hand.

---

8. Earl Jabay, *The Kingdom of Self* (Plainfield, N.J.: Logos International, 1974), p. 48.

Since guilt is a painful feeling, we can unknowingly disguise it and hide it from our conscious minds. By pushing it into the subconscious, we avoid the pain and consider ourselves free from it. But our inner restlessness and emotional lives betray us, for we continue to be troubled by inner conflicts and frustrations as the repressed guilt sneaks out under other names.[9]

In spite of our "enlightened society," our "new morality," and the "psychological maturity" of our "New Age" movement, we are still plagued by guilt. But we don't call it guilt. We have substituted a new vocabulary and a new code for it. Parents and teachers who used to call children "good" or "bad" now say they are "mature" or "immature," "adjusted" or "maladjusted." What we actually feel, however, if we aren't "mature" or "well adjusted" is still that old sense of guilt. In a world plagued by personal frustrations and attended by an army of mental health professionals, many of us are still looking for relief from a nameless anxiety without realizing that our basic problem is guilt.[10]

The paralysis of guilt is all too real. It has put humanity out of control—in rebellion, estrangement, isolation, and alienation. Our performance is in error; we are missing the mark. Our selves are out of control because we have no standard by which we can measure ourselves. How can we know when we're in or out of control? What are we in rebellion against, in estrangement, in isolation, or alienation from? Where is our performance in error, and what is the mark we are missing? If there is no standard of morality or values or universal "should," then there is no guilt. And if there is no guilt, then who has pulled off this guilt-trip hoax that every civilization from time immemorial has experienced?

The problem with the "hoax" theory is that no matter what we call guilt, some sense of "should" gnaws away at us and eventually disintegrates our personness. The paralysis of guilt continues to immobilize and destroy us. Our search for a stan-

9. Bill Counts and Bruce Narramore, *Guilt and Freedom* (Santa Ana, Calif.: Vision House Publishers, 1974), p. 8.
10. Counts and Narramore, pp. 8, 9.

dard will go on, therefore, and the moral questions of right and wrong will persist.

Three major struggles in life are set up by the deadly triad of fear, anger, and guilt. The paralysis of fear sets us up for the struggle of *inadequacy*—"Am I doing something worthwhile in my world?" The paralysis of anger forces us to struggle for *intimacy*—"How do I relate successfully with my most significant relationships?" The paralysis of guilt forces us to struggle for *identity*—"Why am I?" and "Who am I?" We all must grapple with these questions. We cannot ignore them. It seems natural to enter into these struggles.

Paralysis of	leads to	Problem of
FEAR	——————————————————>	INADEQUACY
ANGER	——————————————————>	INTIMACY
GUILT	——————————————————>	IDENTITY

It's like fighting for your own existence. *It's a fight for life.*

Life or Death: A Personal Preference

These struggles for life comprise the essence of what it means to be *hooked on life*. It's basically a choice. You can choose life or death. You can choose to fight for your life—clawing, kicking, screaming, and doing whatever must be done in order to embrace it! Or you can choose death. Obviously, only a few people actually choose death. But *not* making a choice is the same as making a choice—a negative choice. Allowing yourself to be caught up and overcome by the deadly triad of fear, anger, and guilt is to choose death. To refuse to struggle against the problems of inadequacy, lack of intimacy, and loss of identity is to opt for death! Many people (for all practical purposes) die at age thirty-five or thirty-six, and we bury them at seventy-two or seventy-three! Everyone has a choice—to be *stuck in a death cycle* or to be *hooked on a life cycle*.

Learning to Live Life on Purpose

Do you want an alternative to living with pressure? Immediate death and burial! None of us can be hermetically sealed off from the piles of pressure in life. Even though we can't avoid the piles of life, we can definitely avoid becoming a pile ourselves by processing the pressure and avoiding getting stuck.

We process the pressure by learning to live life with a purpose. We make life happen rather than wait for it to happen. We can process life three ways. We have three positive choices, no matter what our economic level or vocation. These universal processes will positively affect us, in both our most intimate relationships and our businesses. These universal processes enable us to make life work best for us—even in the midst of the pressure-cooker!

1. Process of Achieving: How to Be Responsible

This is the most emphasized process. "What are you going to do when you grow up?" "What do you want to be?" The bombardment of questions such as these begins at the earliest level of understanding and continues through university level. (A few years later many of us again ask ourselves these same questions so that we may enjoy a proper mid-life crisis!)

The process of achieving attempts to solve the problem of inadequacy. It is the struggle for self-worth. Are we doing anything worthwhile? Are we able to make a significant mark on our world?

The key word for the process of achieving is *responsibility*. Instead of waiting for life just to happen, we take the responsibility to make it happen! In order to achieve successfully, we must exercise personal responsibility. We assume responsibility *for* ourselves and *to* everyone else.

In the process of achieving, however, we hit upon two depressing thoughts that also help clarify the need for personal responsibility as a way of life.

Depressing Thought One: *No one in this life cares as much as you do about what you are doing. Nobody.*

If you aren't in a total depression yet, try **Depressing**

Thought Two: *If anything is going to be achieved in your life, you must do it. Only you.*

Responsibility! It's the only way to function positively in the process of achieving. But as important as this first process is, it cannot stand alone. Though many of us try to make the process of achieving our primary focus in life, our kingdoms ultimately crumble if achieving is our foundation.

Problem of	⟶	Life process of	⟶	Key function
INADEQUACY		ACHIEVING		RESPONSIBILITY

2. Process of Relating: How to Be Relational

Being masters of surface relationships, we have created a desperate problem—a loss of intimacy. The struggle for intimacy is painful. If the pain from past relational failures doesn't put a halt to intimacy, then the painful fear of a new relationship will.

The key word here is *relationship.* Relationships demand active interest and maintenance, or death is inevitable.

Relationships are extremely powerful! They can drag us down to despair or boost us toward our greatest fulfillment. When relationships work, life seems to work best, even in the worst of times. The process of achieving is enhanced by the process of relating. And the processes of achieving and relating are based upon the process of becoming.

Problem of	⟶	Life process of	⟶	Key function
INTIMACY		RELATING		RELATIONSHIP

3. Process of Becoming: How to Be Realistic

Because the process of becoming is the least understood, it is usually given the weakest emphasis. From childhood we are asked, "What are you going to do when you grow up?" Or possibly, "Who are your friends?" But rarely does anyone encourage us to understand our identity by asking, "Who are you?"

The process of becoming attempts to solve the problem of identity. The identity crisis is for real and affects us all. We all must try to find ourselves.

The key word for the process of becoming is *reality,* yet we rarely welcome reality as a friend. Most of us would rather be told what we want to hear, not what we need to hear. Reality is neither the way things appear to be nor the way we wish them to be. Reality is the way things actually are. As a bumper sticker put it: "Reality is only for those who can't cope with drugs!"

Reality isn't easy, but the process of becoming requires a healthy dose of it and provides the foundational process of life. When this is true, our lives are rooted in reality!

Problem of ⎯⎯⎯⎯→ Life process of ⎯⎯⎯⎯→ Key function
IDENTITY   BECOMING   REALITY

Watch Out for People-Tracks. All three processes of life—achieving, relating, and becoming—are necessary for life to work best. We can see how this works by comparing life to railroad tracks. A train requires two tracks in order to get anywhere. If it leaves the tracks, it topples over and gets stuck. Trains must run on tracks or they won't work. We are the same way, except we require three tracks (achieving, relating, and becoming). We may try to jump the tracks, but if we allow ourselves to be derailed, we get just as stuck as the trackless train. Life won't work without our three people-tracks!

If all three tracks are not used, derailment is inevitable. I see this in my own life when I try to balance only on the track of achieving. It's so easy for me to get caught up in my work. I love what I do, yet the work never ends. As I try to operate on only one track, the other two slip out of focus, and I neglect the tracks of becoming and relating. I charge ahead, wondering why I'm dissatisfied. But the dissatisfaction is inevitable. People *must* function on all three people-tracks to be happy. There is no other way. (Each of these people-tracks, or processes, will be discussed more fully later.)

⎯→ INADEQUACY ⎯→ ACHIEVING ⎯→ RESPONSIBILITY ⎯→
⎯→ INTIMACY ⎯⎯→ RELATING ⎯→ RELATIONSHIP ⎯→
⎯→ IDENTITY ⎯⎯→ BECOMING ⎯→ REALITY ⎯⎯⎯→

Stuck on Our Way to Life. Life's major problem is to keep ourselves on track. If only life were not so complex. Because of this complexity, we try to travel along in life only to find ourselves stuck. Not just once, but many times in our journey. Frustration overwhelms us because most of us have no clear-cut understanding of how to get unstuck. I once saw an interesting piece of graffiti that expressed this attitude. Someone had drawn a radio with a message coming out of the speaker. The message said: "This life is a test. It is only a test. Had this been an actual life, you would have received instructions as to what to do and where to go."

Our problem is that we haven't been told who we are, how to relate, and how to achieve. We have been given a few clues but no full instructions on how to live life. On the way to living life the best way we know how, we get stuck, stuck on work, alcohol, drugs, sex, food (too much or too little), smoking, negative relationships, anger, guilt, divorce, handicaps, disease, or loneliness.

We get stuck on our way to living life. Anything that keeps us from living life to its fullest will get us stuck. All of us become stuck at some point in the process of living. And in the midst of being stuck we all have two choices: (1) *"hang in there" and stay stuck,* or (2) *admit that we are stuck and do what we must to start over!*

We *must* know who we are, where we are going, and how to relate to other people. If we get derailed from one of the three people-tracks, we get stuck in life's pressures. The following story makes this clear.

A distraught, suicidal man went to see a psychiatrist. He was desperate. He poured out his deep anguish, pain, and loneliness to the psychiatrist. He said he wanted to kill himself. The psychiatrist listened intently as the man talked about his disappointments and failures.

When the man stopped speaking, he looked expectantly at the psychiatrist. The psychiatrist said, "I want to recommend something that is a bit out of the ordinary, but I think it could help. I have heard that a clown is performing at the theater downtown. I hear that people are rolling in the aisles and that their laughter can be heard from blocks away. I recommend that you buy a ticket, attend that show, and see that clown. I have a hunch that you too will get caught up in the laughter and enjoyment and discover that life is still worth living."

The man looked down. "I can't go see that clown."

"Why?" the psychiatrist asked. "Why won't you give it a try? Why not be a part of life before you try to end it?"

The man wept, "I can't go see that clown. I am that clown."

A lot of us are made up to look good and act happy. We try to please the entire world, and in the process we end up empty, alone, and desperate. We get stuck because we get derailed from the three people-tracks, the three processes of life—becoming, relating, and achieving. But we can start over. If we are willing to try, there is hope. We *can* live life with a purpose.

The World of the Obsessed

It was Sunday morning, and once again Stanton Campbell pulled up in front of the church in his polished red sports car. The car was impeccable in appearance. The Porsche 911 reflected Stanton's image of the ideal American male.

Stanton, a thirty-two-year-old public relations executive, along with the beautiful blonde woman he had been seeing for the last three weeks, was making his regular appearance at church. Stanton rarely missed a Sunday. Church attendance promoted Stanton's image of "a beautiful human being."

Stanton was the picture of health and strength. He even taught a physical fitness class at a local health club. His body couldn't have been in better shape. Many people thought he was *the* man to be seen with. No other bachelor could offer so much. His car, his home, and his clothes told the world that he was a man of means, that he could command the finer things of life.

His newest companion, the prettiest of six he had brought to church in the past six months, was the secretary of his newest client. He had met Marsha on his first call to her office. When he saw her, it was as if his heart had melted. Instantly he was in love. Marsha was the finest woman he had ever met. She would be different from the others, he thought. She would live up to his greatest expectations.

But of course she could not meet his expectations. She, like all the rest, would fall far short of meeting Stanton's criterion of total perfection. In the process, she would verify once again to Stanton that he could attract, conquer, and dispose of the best, at his own convenience. To Stanton a new woman was like a new sports coat. Wear it, receive compliments on it, and when you tire of it or find a nicer one, dispose of it and begin wearing the new object of affection.

On the outside, Stanton appeared to have it all together. On the inside, however, Stanton lived in the world of the obsessed. He was obsessed by his own feelings of inferiority. Not measuring up to others' expectations plagued him the most. Spending was a major form of compensation for Stanton. His compulsive buying sprees ended with clothes he did not want, electronic toys he did not need, and bills he did not want to pay. His possessions made him feel valuable, while his obsession with inferiority made him feel worthless. His entire world was saturated with various forms of compensation for his obsession with inferiority. As a result, the man of seeming perfection who looked so good was isolated by empty possessions and hollow relationships. At age thirty-two, life was passing Stanton Campbell by.

Stanton was also a religious fanatic. He talked about God throughout the day, took up the offering as an usher at church, and rarely missed a Sunday. He even had a little fish put on the back of his car to indicate he was a Christian. Women found his statements of belief in God and his desire to be at church on Sunday refreshing. It hooked them into believing that he was different, that he was ideal. Although nothing was wrong with what he did, something was very wrong with *why* he did these things. His talk and his attendance at church were in direct conflict with the way he *lived* his life.

This direct conflict caused a bizarre cycle of private behavior. Stanton used his religiosity as part of his attack-and-conquer strategy.

It was common for him to invite a new woman to his home and eventually into the bedroom to kneel beside the bed for prayer. It was also common for Stanton to be lying under the covers with the same woman thirty minutes later. This ritual worked well for Stanton. When he could persuade a female to cross the psychological barrier into the bedroom ostensibly to pray, it was easier for Stanton to persuade her to return when he had other motives. Although this tactic worked for Stanton, it produced extreme guilt. Had Stanton reflected on his compulsive sexual behavior and asked himself, "Why am I doing this?" he might also have asked, "What am I trying to prove?" Those two questions could then have led him into realizing that, for him, his bizarre behavior came from his deep sense of inferiority.

On the outside Stanton appeared to be a faithful believer. The genuine people of God who attended church to worship would never have guessed his church attendance was actually the deception Stanton practiced to survive. Survival was difficult for Stanton. Like all people living in the world of the obsessed, he was visited frequently by confusion, anxiety, and desperation.

Stanton Campbell was *stuck* in a world of obsessions, trapped by compulsions and unresolved guilt. Guilt ate at his ego and left him feeling inferior. The man who looked great to the world felt terrible inside.

Stanton Campbell is but one of many who live with obsessive thoughts and compulsive acts. The most renowned case of obsession, perhaps, was Howard Hughes. The television movie about him portrayed how his daily compulsive routines centered around his obsession with cleanliness. He fought to avoid contact with people to minimize exposure to the germs he so greatly detested. Even in his last days, when he was too weak to walk to the restroom, he used tissue paper and gloves to separate himself from those who carried him. While we can speculate about the emotions that drove him to obsessive, compulsive behavior, we probably shall never know about them with any degree of certainty.

Classic literature abounds with characters whose lives were full of obsessions and compulsions. Shakespeare portrayed the tyranny of obsession through the character of Lady Macbeth. At one point she walks in her sleep, wringing her hands as if to wash them. As she repeats this ritualistic compulsion, she pleads, "Out, out, damned spot." Lady Macbeth is obsessed with feelings of uncleanness, of contamination. She is trapped in the common compulsion of hand washing. And beneath it all is the unresolved emotion of guilt. She had participated in the death plot of the king and then had touched the bloodstained knives that killed him.

Whether it's Lady Macbeth, Howard Hughes, or Stanton Campbell, we see people who are stuck. They are stuck in the world of the obsessed, a world full of meaningless and destructive compulsions. They feel hopeless. They want out, but they feel there is no way. But there *is* a way out. The journey out leads to hope and serenity. The journey is best entered early, however, before the obsessed get stuck in compulsive, failure-ridden lives.

Obsessions: Inner Space Invaders

Obsessions are intrusive thoughts that invade the mind, especially when such thoughts are not wanted. These repetitive thoughts return day after day to haunt people and drive them toward destruction. Mental hospitals are full of the extreme cases where people have lost control due to their obsessions. But more commonly, the obsessed are freely walking around outside, appearing to be quite normal.

Obsessions that invade the conscious thinking, much to the discomfort of the invaded, include power, control, failure, inferiority, money, death, and success. Although this list is not exhaustive, it includes many obsessions familiar to a vast number of people. Although they differ in intensity, common threads are obvious in most obsessions. Power, success, money, and control are positive images, while failure, inferiority, and death are negative images that oppose the positive. In actuality, they are reverse variations of the same obsessive theme.

The obsessive theme is *self*. Haunting questions emerge in the form of, "What am *I* going to become?" "Who will *I* be?" "How can *I* be more?" "Why do *I* feel so small?" "How can *I* overcome?" The self is in shambles, and obsessions confirm the destruction.

Those who are plagued by obsessions often feel they are living in a misplaced world. No matter what they do or where they turn, their discomfort remains and their obsessions continue.

Anxiety. Obsessions produce great discomfort in those who experience them. They sap people of their energy and vitality. They drain the creative reserves. They leave people frustrated from relentless thoughts that increase in intensity in proportion to the fight to stifle them.

Ambivalence. Obsessions generate conflicting feelings. Ambivalence is a characteristic of those who are obsessed, desirous of relief and change, yet never knowing what to do or where to turn. Most are tired of everyone else's "home remedies" that just never seem to work.

Mental Confusion. Obsessions interfere with the way the brain functions. They can rob people of their memories. They can distort judgment and cause great errors in decision making. At times they can destroy all mental functioning.

Emotions: Behind the Scenes

Behind these repetitive thoughts called obsessions are some very basic unresolved emotions. The base for all the obsessions is formed by three unresolved emotions: guilt, fear, and anger.

1. Guilt: When the Past Is Unresolved

Guilt can be either appropriate or inappropriate. Appropriate guilt occurs when we do something in direct conflict with our system of values. For example, if we believe in the rights of an individual and yet steal, we feel guilty after stealing. That is appropriate guilt. Another example: when the commitment of marriage is broken because one partner is involved in an affair, the guilt that same partner feels is appropriate.

Inappropriate guilt comes from events beyond our control. When parents divorce, children feel a high level of inappropriate guilt because they feel that they are responsible. Such guilt often plagues children for years. Victims of incest who remain silent and cover up the event will suffer years of inappropriate guilt over something they couldn't help.

Appropriate or inappropriate, if guilt is unresolved, it results in obsessions of the mind. Stanton Campbell could not recognize his problem as unresolved guilt. He could not identify his inferiority feelings as a product of guilt. At best, he saw himself only as somewhat more selfish than he should be. But in reality, behind it all is the unresolved guilt from all of his conflicting behaviors.

Unresolved guilt can show up in many ways. In Stanton's case, it produced haunting obsessions. Below are some obsessions frequently manifested from unresolved guilt:

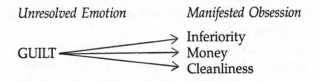

Unresolved Emotion   *Manifested Obsession*

GUILT → Inferiority
→ Money
→ Cleanliness

2. Fear: When Anxiety Is Unfocused

Fear can be experienced as extreme terror or as frequent attacks of free-floating anxiety, the kind that has no specific focus but leaves us with a general dread or uneasiness about life. The source of fear can be either realistic or unrealistic, as with guilt. Whatever the source or type, if fear is unresolved, a whole different set of obsessions can surface.

If we are in a state of constant fear and anxiety, we might have a nagging sense of failure, or we might continue to focus on the measure of our success. But rarely can we identify fear as the root of our problem.

Some obsessions manifested from unresolved fear include:

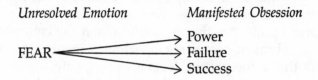

Unresolved Emotion   *Manifested Obsession*

FEAR → Power
→ Failure
→ Success

3. Anger: When Expectations Are Unmet

Anger can result from unmet expectations. Angry people are needy people. They have either cheated themselves or feel that they have been cheated. Anger destroys the ability to relate because the focus is always on the person who has failed to meet the other's expectations.

Anger toward a parent is quite common as a source of unresolved emotion. I was quite angry with my own father for some time because of my unmet expectations. I felt that he should have provided more money, a better house, and newer cars. I resented his lack of material wealth. I was angry because I wanted more and he provided less.

One day I tried to explain to a counselor how I was not resentful, angry, or bitter toward my father. He allowed me to finish before confronting me with evidence that my anger had been brewing for years. With this counselor's help, I was able to accept and deal with my anger and then focus on what my father *had* provided. When I was able to think in terms of my dad's strengths rather than his weaknesses, my unresolved anger began to subside. Unrealistic and unmet expectations faded as love and respect for him grew. Resolving my anger provided an emotional freedom that I had not felt in years.

We can see anger in all kinds of situations. A man walks out on his family. As a result, his teen-aged daughter feels great anger. He has failed to fulfill her expectations of fatherhood. This anger, if not resolved, can become an obsession that makes her think of him as dead or dying. Or her obsessive thoughts might dwell on death in general, but deep within, the unresolved anger has found its outlet in this form.

Some obsessions manifested from unresolved anger are:

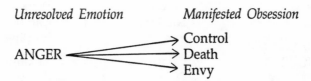

Unresolved Emotion	Manifested Obsession
ANGER	Control
	Death
	Envy

Of course a person can experience one or all three of these unresolved emotions. At the same time, a person may have multiple obsessions. *The greater the intensity of the problem and the longer it has persisted, the more complex the emotion-obsession relationships will be.*

In addition, what manifests from one unresolved emotion for one person may be entirely different for someone else. Guilt may surface as an obsession with money for one person, with cleanliness for another. Or guilt may produce feelings of inferiority. As with Stanton Campbell, he fell short of his own expectations to act in accordance with his established values.

Guilt, fear, and anger form the base for a life out of control.

But the haunting obsessions that crop up are only a part of the total pattern of discomfort. These combinations result in compulsions.

Compulsions: The Acts That Must Be Performed

Whereas obsessions are repeated thoughts, compulsions are repeated acts that must be performed as a result of the obsessions. These repeated acts may be trivial and ritualistic, as in the case of incessant hand washing, or they may be immediately devastating, as in the case of heavy gambling or excessive spending.

Below are common compulsive acts, matched with possible obsessions that may be causing them. In addition, the unresolved emotions that form the base of the problem are shown.

Unresolved Emotion	Manifested Obsession	Resulting Compulsion
GUILT	Inferiority	Drinking
	Money	Spending
	Cleanliness	Hand washing
FEAR	Power	Work
	Failure	Gambling
	Success	Stealing
ANGER	Control	Talking
	Death	Eating
	Envy	Stealing

How Stanton Campbell Was Snagged by the Trap

The combination of unresolved emotions, manifested obsessions, and resulting compulsions forms a trap that snags us in deeper over time. We can break out of the trap, but we can't break out alone. Here is how the trap was set and repeated itself in the case of Stanton Campbell.

Stanton Campbell's mother was killed in a tragic traffic accident at 9:00 P.M. one Friday when he was fourteen. The man driving her car was not Stanton's father. He was unknown to

Stanton and Stanton's father. When the facts were made known, Mrs. Campbell had been having an affair for over six months. Several weeks later, Stanton's dad told him that his mother had the affair because of the great pressure she had felt from the family. Stanton was struck with intense guilt. He felt that it was all somehow his fault. His guilt was never resolved.

Stanton carried the guilt with him through adolescence. As a result he felt he was never good enough. It was as if everyone else had life wrapped up except him. He felt inferior to everyone around him. His feelings of inferiority drove him to achieve and acquire. He worked hard and bought hard. Everything he did was done with a vengeance to overcome and outdo. But when he compulsively spent too much, his unresolved guilt painfully surfaced. This only added to his compulsivity.

The girls he dated were victims of the trap he was in. He sought them out of his desire to feel superior. But once he had conquered them sexually, he felt so guilty that he would end the relationship. Then he moved on to someone else, hoping that it would be different, but always repeating the past. Unresolved guilt, leading to inferiority, leading to compulsions to spend, conquer, and look and talk religious, kept Stanton Campbell trapped in a world of the obsessed.

This world entraps many. We can't escape alone; we need help from others. But for Stanton and all the rest of us in similar traps, *the process of getting out begins with accepting that there is a problem and admitting that if it could be handled alone, the problem would have already been resolved.*

In the case of Lady Macbeth, guilt had led to an obsession with cleanliness that resulted in compulsive hand washing. Other examples of unresolved emotion-obsession-compulsion are as easily tracked. Fear can lead to an obsession with success that can result in stealing. Acquiring of goods is an attempt to look successful. Looking successful compensates for the intense fear. The consequences of theft secure the trap. Once the theft is committed, the fear of being caught or found out feeds the obsession with success and the drive to steal again.

People with unresolved anger may become obsessed with control—control of situations and of other people's time. One compulsion that results, for example, may be nonstop talking. Nonstop talkers are not making an effort to communicate but an effort to be in control. The trap is set for that person because people tend to avoid others who talk in order to maintain control of a conversation. The subsequent rejection only intensifies the anger of the person obsessed with control.

Addiction is another complication that entraps the victims of obsessions and compulsions. Addiction is a misunderstood concept. It is not caused by obsessions and compulsions, but obsessions and compulsions can result in certain behaviors that are potentially addictive. For instance, guilt may lead to drinking, and drinking is potentially addictive. But only one person in ten becomes addicted to alcohol because alcohol is a selectively addictive chemical. Some people simply cannot drink enough to enter the addiction process. So although the obsession may lead to the potentially addictive chemical, the obsession doesn't cause the addiction. The addiction is caused by the chemical and the individual's biological predisposition.

A parallel to the predisposition to alcohol addiction would be diabetes. Obsessions may lead to compulsive eating of foods with high sugar content. But diabetes occurs only when intake of sugar is combined with a human body susceptible to the disease. Again, as in the case of alcoholism, the problem is caused by the combination of a chemical and the individual's biological predisposition.

The addiction trap is one of the most difficult problems. If a person is experiencing obsessions and compulsions and simultaneously becomes addicted to a drug, the obsessions and compulsions will intensify. The addicted drinker is able to drink more with fewer results because of the buildup of tolerance, a characteristic of an addictive chemical. If the tolerance increases and the supply decreases, anxiety and more compulsive behaviors result.

In alcoholism treatment centers, it is not unusual for those who stop drinking to start another compulsive behavior to replace it. It is common for a nonsmoker to start smoking or an existing smoker to double the amount smoked. Many patients begin eating uncontrollably—and if you've ever tasted food served at most treatment centers, you know that increased eating is an unusual phenomenon!

The central point of the addiction trap is that it complicates and magnifies problems that already exist. Not all compulsive drinkers become addicted, but when it does happen, the intensity of other compulsive acts is bound to increase.

The Miserable State of Obsession

The life of an obsessed individual is characterized by some commonalities. Together, these commonalities or systems combine to form the state of obsession. These seven symptoms are earmarks of misery as a result of obsessions and compulsions.

1. Emotional Turmoil: The Child Inside

In this state are found guilt and anger over the past. In fact, these emotions often keep the person rooted to the past. Although the past may be full of pain and disappointment, it becomes the focal point for the person living in the state of obsession.

One reason for the focus on the past is fear and anxiety about the future. The person often compensates with an outer shell of overconfidence. But down inside is a frightened child afraid of what tomorrow may bring. Unresolved emotional turmoil makes the present almost unbearable in the state of obsession. For the person in this state, retreating to the past seems the only alternative.

2. Illusions: The Great Cover-Up

The state of obsession is filled with illusions. For entertainment we pay people to produce fantastic illusions. These magicians spend their lives making us believe that something that is not there, really is, and in turn they make us believe that what is present, really is not.

In the state of obsession, the person attempts the role of magician in his or her life. This person comes up with gross exaggerations and specific lies to build the illusion of success. The great cover-up of personal flaws feeds an unbelievable image of perfection. The obsessed individual eventually leads a life that is a total lie made difficult because of an inability to distinguish the lie from reality. Illusions are anything but entertaining for a person in the state of obsession.

3. Alienation: An Army of One

Alienation and total isolation accompany the obsessed state. The person feels that the struggle to survive must be fought alone. Accompanying this are feelings of being misplaced or out of place. The alienated long for a geographical change in order to find a place to belong. For a person in the state of obsession, belonging does not occur.

4. Discomfort: Head of Complaint Department

Constant complaining is characteristic of individuals fighting obsessions and compulsions. Everything becomes an excuse for complaining. Nothing or no one is good enough. Everything falls far short of satisfying. It is a miserable state, and family members are always asking themselves, "What have I done wrong?" The reason they ask the question of themselves is that the obsessed person is never happy with them or what they do.

5. Pressure: Tyranny of the "Shoulds"

In this state the person has no concept of needs. The entire world revolves around the struggle of doing what "should" be done. Most of the time, the consideration is for what will promote the false image of having it together. The person is constantly thinking about what "should" be done to look "good," talk "right," or be in the "best" place, rather than thinking of personal needs and the needs of others.

Often these "shoulds" come from the past and are attempts to compensate for unresolved emotions. Frequently a person is acting today in an attempt to please someone from the past— even if that someone may have died 20 years ago.

People tryannized by the "shoulds" live their lives by trying harder and harder. And rather than reach their desires, they achieve only more frustration and agony over what "should" be done. "Shoulds" from the past rule over needs of the present.

6. Emptiness: A Hole in the Gut

This whole lifestyle leaves the person with a deep sense of personal emptiness, a hole-in-the-gut sensation. The person feels that much is missing from life, that he or she is incomplete.

This emptiness often will lead to a greater number of compulsions, as vain attempts are made to fill the void. But more drugs, more spending, more gambling never do the job. The feeling of emptiness grows greater as more and more attempts to fill it prove futile.

7. Despair: A Home for Many

Despair sums up the entire state of obsession. The person repeats desperate attempts to make life work, but nothing works. The harder the person tries, the greater the despair. The trying and fighting are done alone, and that only increases the despair.

Some people who are desperate try suicide as the final cure to their lonely, empty pain that grows deeper. They reach this point after they have tried other solutions and failed. Those close to the person are left with their own guilt and anger over not being able to help.

In summary, people in a state of obsession have a miserable existence. They have little or no self-esteem, yet they project a picture of total confidence. They are driven by excessive expectations that are rarely met. Over time, the self-discipline that was once a source of pride to them is completely shattered.

Their lives are a parade of extremes. They move from prohibition to permissiveness on a daily basis. They may deprive themselves of food all day only to gorge themselves at night. They may stop drinking for a month and then stay drunk for days. They may be kind and caring people one moment and then only moments later become violent from a seething rage that festers inside.

The state of obsession is where many live and few escape. But there is a way out. It is a tried and true method of moving on to a state of serenity and peace. But it is not easy.

Where's the Exit from Obsessions?

If you talk to people whose lives are riddled with obsessions and compulsions, you will most likely hear stories about tremendous effort and attempts to change. Every story is filled with strong motivation, a short period of hope, then a return to the problem. The fact is, *trying harder does not produce the desired result of long-term change.*

You also may hear about lengthy psychiatric sessions that were terminated just when some progress was being made. Desperation drives people to seek help in developing some insight into their constant discomfort. But because insight alone is not the answer, they stop going to their sessions.

You would also hear stories about stopping one compulsion only to start up another one. Everyone is familiar with the weight gain that usually accompanies the termination of smoking. Merely stopping one compulsive behavior only results in creating a problem of a different nature. Frequently a person ends up stuck with two problems rather than just the original one. If someone had asked Lady Macbeth to stop wringing her hands, she most likely would have started chain smoking or overeating or brought some other repeated trivial behavior to the surface. *Just changing or stopping the compulsion does nothing to resolve the obsessions of the mind and the unresolved emotions.*

The journey out of the state of obsession begins with the willingness to do whatever it takes, which is different from searching for the easiest solution. Convenience rarely has a place in doing whatever it takes. But a person tired of being driven by obsessions and frustrated with compulsions that increase their grip eventually must reach the willingness to do whatever it takes.

This level of willingness involves one or a combination of tough steps on the journey out of the obsessions. It will involve a time of intensive in-patient treatment of thirty days or more for many people, especially those with alcohol, drug, or eating disorder problems. It may involve several meetings a week at Alcoholics Anonymous, Narcotics Anonymous, or some other self-help group. It definitely will involve a long-term commitment to at least one other person which is for the purpose of developing accountability to another individual. In this relationship of accountability, there must be a growing degree of both honesty and openness—honesty about the problem and openness in sharing it. The relationship may need to be with a therapist or some other professional.

More will be presented later on the recovery process, and a multidimensional plan toward total wellness will be laid out. The plan for total wellness will include the dimensions of becoming, relating, and achieving. But for now, it is essential to look at the absence or presence of this willingness factor. When it is present, the journey toward the state of serenity and peace begins.

The State of Serenity and Peace: A New Home

The opposite of the state of obsession is the state of serenity and peace. People in the state of obsession search for, but rarely experience, serenity and peace. The state of serenity and peace is not some boring existence where we hum and contemplate our navels. It is, instead, a lifestyle full of purpose and vibrancy. It is existence with meaning.

The key elements of serenity and peace are emotional stability, reality, relationships, comfort, search for the best, wholeness, and hope.

1. Emotional Stability: Feeling Secure in the Present

Stability results from resolving all of the garbage from the past that feeds the reservoirs of guilt, fear, and anger. With the past resolved, we have an accompanying feeling of assurance for the future. This is not overconfidence; instead, it is the knowledge that the future is manageable. Having the future assured and the past resolved allows us to have a feeling of security in the present. The prospects of the moment offer great satisfaction. Delusional concepts of past and future are swept away as the living for today guides us along the desired path of the future, one day at a time. In a state of serenity and peace, the present is not such a bad place to live. In fact, it is enough.

2. Reality: Controlling Life as It Is

Reality is foreign territory to the obsessed. The obsessed seek to distort reality and find that in the end, the distortions are more difficult to handle than reality itself.

The need to create illusions is gone from peace and serenity. Reality is good enough. Nothing more, nothing less. Reality, combined with life in the present, is the easiest form of life to manage. At times it is quite painful, yet through the pain we make progress toward resolution and enjoy the ability to remain in control.

3. Relationships: Enjoying Life with Others

Serenity and peace move us from fighting the world alone to enjoying life with others. It is the end of self-inflicted alienation. Growth occurs, but not the type of growth that leaves others behind. It is the type of growth that stimulates and motivates others to grow also.

Without relationships, we merely exist. In a state of serenity and peace, relationships move us from existence into multi-dimensional living where sharing experiences becomes the goal. The act of sharing overrides the egotistical alienation that cries out, "Let me do it alone!" Doing it alone is still possible but not necessary. Strong relationships grow stronger with time. To *see* the sunset is to experience beauty. To *share* a sunset is to experience a beautiful life.

4. Comfort: Focusing on the Positive

In a state of peace and serenity, no one is a victim. We may be victimized from time to time, as in the case of being robbed, but we do not remain victims. Peace and serenity are derived from accepting the grossly unfair aspects of reality and living comfortably with them.

Peace and serenity are maintained by looking for the positive and good in others. It is a process of continually refocusing off the negative. As we continue this practice, we develop an immense ability to find comfort in the worst of situations. It is anything but waiting around for others to provide our happiness.

5. Search for the Best: Meeting Needs

When we move to a state of serenity and peace, we return to meeting needs rather than remaining tyrannized by "shoulds" from a distant past. And this meeting of needs maintains the delicate balance of meeting personal needs as well as meeting the needs of others.

In searching for what is best, we return to the values of life. No longer does immediate gratification dictate our decisions. Discipline, commitment and responsibility take precedence over what feels the best or is the easiest at the moment.

As we search for the best, we eventually seek a knowledge of God. There is no room for atheists here. Meaning of life is established from a spiritual perspective grounded in a growing knowledge and awareness of God.

The search for the best always results in increasing levels of maturity. Maturity never indicates arrival; rather, it indicates continuing personal growth. Although maturity is different for each of us, it is obvious when present in our lives. Its presence is recognized in the search for the best, and it transcends what is merely good or satisfactory.

6. Wholeness: A Sense of Completion

In place of agonizing emptiness, we experience a growing wholeness as we experience serenity and peace. Emptiness is replaced with purpose and direction which surround every aspect of our lives. Becoming, relating, and achieving do not occur in isolation or by chance. They happen as an integral part of a plan toward an ultimate goal.

No one thing or activity ever makes us feel whole. Wholeness comes from the balanced integration of physical, mental, emotional, social, and spiritual components of life. As the search for the best and growth continue, a base of satisfaction is derived from these five dimensions working in harmony together.

For example, religious fanatics place value in pseudo-spiritual growth where both social and mental dimensions suffer. Because this is a one-dimensional process of growth, wholeness never flourishes. Coordination of growth leads to a sense of completion and being whole.

7. Hope: The Greatest Motivator

Hope is by far the most significant aspect of serenity and peace. It makes life worth getting up for. Despair has no room when hope is present. The two simply cannot exist together. Hope lends itself to growth. We can be willing to experience pain because we realize that it will subside eventually. Hope does not take away pain. Hope makes pain give way to greater insight and maturity.

If we could name just one item most valuable for the person stuck in the mire of obsessions and compulsions, it is hope. Hope is the greatest motivator through rough times. And the greatest characteristic of hope is its availability to everyone.

Check Yourself Out

The chart below illustrates how the state of obsessions contrasts directly and specifically with the state of serenity and peace.

Obsessions	Serenity and Peace
Emotional turmoil	Emotional stability
Illusions	Reality
Alienation	Relationships
Discomfort	Comfort
Pressure	Search for the best
Emptiness	Wholeness
Despair	Hope

If we identify more closely with the elements of the left-hand column, it is a good indicator that we are living in a state of obsession. The object is to become willing to do whatever it takes to produce movement toward the concepts of the right-hand column. Even though there is never a point at which we finally arrive, our goal is the process of growth.

Yet many don't attempt to move from obsessions to serenity and peace. Why? The most frequent problem is the unwillingness to pay the price for growth to occur. Most of us who recognize the need want change to occur immediately, with no pain. But obsessions don't emerge overnight, and neither does growth.

Delusional thinking is another problem that often prevents us from accepting the seriousness of our situation. Confrontation from someone else is at times the only thing that wakes us up to reality. Even when we are made aware, our tendency is to place temporary solutions in front of serious problems. It is no different from putting a small bandage on a deep wound.

Some lives need major surgery in every area, and paralysis has set in from unresolved injuries in the past. But help is possible. The scalpel of honesty wielded by the surgeon of time begins the operation of healing. Waiting at the end of the process is the greatest motivator of all—hope for a life full of meaning and purpose. *Hope is available to anyone who is willing to do whatever it takes.*

Survival Roles of a Codependent Family: In Balance but Out of Joint

Janet dragged Bob into a counselor's office one dreary, rainy morning. Janet complained that Bob was grossly overweight, drank too much beer, paid too little attention to her, and yelled too much at their three kids! The entire family was counseled weekly for nearly three months and then enthusiastically released to enjoy a healthy family life. Bob decided he had been wrong in his behavior, and he learned to change for his own good as well as that of the family.

But within six months a most remarkable shift occurred in this family's problems. Initially Bob was the primary offender, but now he was changed. He lost weight and looked terrific! He cut out his excessive beer guzzling, became more sensitive to Janet, and even began to treat his children like humans! All that she had complained about before was now altered. Bob had been masterful in his life-changes.

It was at exactly this point that Janet fell in love with another man. It was almost as if Janet had suddenly snapped. It seemed to make no difference to her that Bob had been successful in positively changing his behavior toward her and their family. She was bent on running away with her new lover into a fantasy world all her own. No logic in her decision. No reality. Only fantasy.

What caused such a volcanic shift in Janet? Bob's dramatic changes. If Bob had remained a clod, the marriage might have lasted a little longer. Janet was quite comfortable with Bob as a clod. Now that he had changed, she felt extremely uncomfortable. Their marriage was in balance before the change. Now, because Bob had changed and shifted the balance, Janet had to make some changes too. Otherwise, the marriage would be acutely imbalanced and intolerable. That's why she was so driven toward running away with a new lover. She felt starting over was much easier than experiencing the pain of personal change in order to adapt to the new and healthier Bob.

A Family in Balance

Whenever people get stuck—really stuck—most of them have a lineup of relatives and close friends who feel a sense of responsibility. They take on a role that helps those stuck persons survive. By their existence, they bring a balance into the life. The life may then be balanced but still out of joint.

For Every Dependency, There Is an Enabler

First, a couple of definitions. The person who is addicted or dependent is stuck. For every dependent or addicted person there is someone, an enabler, who allows the addiction or dependency to continue. Most of us have played (or are playing) the role of enabling some poor soul to remain stuck. We call these people the chief enablers. (Here's another definition. Enabling is any behavior that allows addicts to continue to function by shielding them from the consequences of their behavior and thereby preventing meaningful recovery.)

How does this work? The enablers help the dependent to deny their problems. It's difficult enough for most people who are stuck to admit their problems, but the enablers make admisson almost impossible. Enablers attempt to change the environment for the dependent in order to keep their problems from openly flaring up. Enablers cover up the addicts' problems as much as possible and protect them from "harmful" consequences.

The chief enabler is normally the person closest to the dependent person. A spouse, parent, doctor, employer, or friend makes an effective enabler. A friend or employer will often cover up absences or will work harder to cover up his or her poor performance. The trusted doctor prescribes drugs to salve the addict's problem rather than solve it. This eases the painful symptoms and encourages the dependent to remain stuck. Without pain, the addict has no motivation to face the problem. Parents loan money, make excuses, and bail their children out of facing the painful consequences of their actions. If parents insist on being responsible for their children instead of encouraging them to be responsible for themselves, then the parents enable the next generation—to be stuck.

In many instances, enabling becomes the chief role of the mate. A husband enables his alcoholic wife by making excuses for her, saying she is sick when she is really drunk. He gets help from an attorney to get her out of jail, *tonight*. He makes excuses for not going to parties. He has two divergent feelings. On the one hand, he fears for the failure of his mate and tries to prevent it. He finds it necessary, therefore, to deny her problem, keeping her put together as his "queen and first lady." On the other hand, he feels great anger toward his wife for falling apart.

The wife also plays the role of the enabler quite effectively. The enabler wife is known as a "saintly" woman. Many times as she gives of herself to help others' hurts, the enabler wife suffers from various physical illnesses. Her main function, nonetheless, is to provide responsibility in the family.

A Family Out of Joint

When children observe their hurting father and their confused and troubled mother in a dependent-codependent relationship, children assume adapted roles for their survival. Thus the family is placed in balance, but at the same time each member is out of joint. Members of this balanced-but-out-of-joint-family can be identified by the kinds of roles they assume.

Superachiever/Family Hero: Saving the Family Name

The superachiever/family hero, usually the oldest child, takes on the role of caretaker of the family. This child is out to save the family name, to make the family proud, to inject the family with a good dose of self-worth.

Outwardly superachievers reflect success, do what is right, exude responsibility, and most of the time live independent lives apart from the family. Inwardly, however, they tend to feel inadequate, hurt, confused, afraid, lonely, and worth little.

The superachievers/family heroes are driven to excel in everything they do. They aim for the top as class president, captain of the basketball team, valedictorian, corporate executive, and social leader. Performance is everything.

Without significant help, superachievers/family heroes will acquire telltale characteristics. They will become workaholics, usually in the helping professions. Tom, the doctor. Edna, the teacher. Nancy, the nurse. Ned, the social worker. They feel responsible for everything! When these children grow up they are least likely to seek professional help. Therefore, the superachievers/family heroes are the toughest to dislodge from their stuckness.

Mascot/Comedian: Laughing Away the Tears

Another child in the codependent family may take on the role of a mascot or comedian. Mascots/comedians represent fun and games to the family system, a sort of comic relief. They normally come across as somewhat fragile, immature, and hyperactive. They're super-cute and humorous; they clown around a lot and will do anything to attract attention. Mascots/comedians divert attention away from the family's pain and problems by the use of humor.

Here we find the typical school clown, company joker, social cutup, or neighborhood prankster. Underneath all the clowning around lies great insecurity. In addition to fear, mascots/comedians feel unloved and unimportant. Unless such family members get help, they'll develop ulcers because of their low stress tolerance. They're driven to be compulsive comics, never staring reality directly in the face. Mascots/comedians are most likely to remain immature the rest of their lives, making life one funny joke. Unfortunately, the punch lines for these life jokes are really not funny, but tragic. Life has passed them by.

Scapegoat/Distractor: Diverting Attention from the Problem

Here is the problem child. No one can deny it! Scapegoats/distractors divert attention away from the family's pain by inappropriate and usually antisocial behavior. They have decided not to compete with the family hero. Since the family usually idolizes the family hero, scapegoats must go outside the family for their needs of belonging and self-worth to be met.

Not only are they out to divert attention away from the family's stuckee-stuckor struggles, but scapegoats/distractors desperately need personal attention. They want to be close to someone, and the only way they know to get family attention is by causing trouble. It is painful, but they welcome the warm strokes of close communication concerning the problem as an adequate trade-off.

Getting into trouble is easy, almost natural, when scapegoats/distractors are closer to an outside "crowd" than to their own family. An unplanned pregnancy will get nine months of attention upon the child and off the main family problem. Scapegoats are troublemakers in school and later on at work. Scapegoats get into drug and alcohol abuse, and many, many times they land in jail.

On the outside scapegoats/distractors are hostile, defiant, withdrawn from traditional society, and antisocial in their talk, dress, and actions. Their primary inner feeling seems to be rejection with all the hurt, anger, loneliness, and jealousy that normally accompany it.

Scapegoats/distractors are sad children. Helping the stuckee-stuckor struggle doesn't help them. They must be treated individually in order to heal their deep-seated sadness.

Quiet/Lost Child: Never Getting Too Close

The quiet/lost child is the forgotten child in the family. This child offers real relief for parents and other family members. He's "one child you'll never have to worry about." She's "such a well-mannered, quiet child."

Lost children are definitely not troublemakers for anyone else, but they're in deeper trouble than anyone ever imagines. They come across as loners, withdrawn, distant, quiet, super-independent. They attach themselves to things, not people. They're followers who have few friends, and they seem almost invisible. They express no needs, and they are rewarded for it. On the inside, lost children are intensely lonely, deeply hurt, greatly confused, and they feel inadequate and unimportant.

The motto of quiet/lost children is: "If you don't get too close you won't get hurt." They're emotionally and relationally deprived. In the future if they get no help, they're in for lives of personal destruction. Sexual identity problems that result in lost children going to one of two extremes—promiscuity or a life all alone—are common. Lost children rarely marry, have little zest for life, and often die young.

Where Are You in the Family Portrait?

The family may be in balance, but each member of the codependent family is disastrously out of joint! Did you see yourself in any of the survival roles? If you have played one of the supporting, survival roles in your family as a child—either as superachiever/hero, mascot/comedian, scapegoat/distractor, or quiet/lost child—there's a high probability that you will perpetuate that role into your family as an adult.

It's easier to play out your "intended" role in the family than it is to upset the balance. No matter how "out of joint" you may feel, there is an intense, almost innate, drive to keep the balance of the codependent family portrait. Unfortunately, the codependent family portrait is a prophecy of disaster after disaster. Without major changes, destruction is inevitable. But you can choose to do something about it.

The Codependent
Family Album

Codependent families usually look good. They look good because they struggle so hard to look good in every action, relationship, and affiliation. We are shocked when we hear that such a family is in trouble. "They appeared so normal!" "Who would have ever thought that *they* had a problem?"

Families that are stuck in survival roles have a knack for fooling people. Their webs of deception are woven so tightly that the family members often fool those closest to the problem, that is, they fool one another. The family masters the art of looking good, while feeling bad. Throughout the troubled family are enormous amounts of bad feelings about one another and about life in general.

Bad feelings piled upon bad feelings leave the troubled family in a state of emotional deprivation. Starved for affection and starved for appreciation, the emotionally starved family members search continually for relief from reality. Their search results in all sorts of behaviors, whether intended consciously or unconsciously, to relieve reality's pain and to fill the void caused by a lack of emotional support and nurturing. Emotional deprivation is real, and its consequences are painful.

The Codependent Family's Source of Protection

Family members, deprived of good, positive feelings about themselves and one another, end up without a language for feelings. They can tell us what they think, they can show us they are angry, but it is next to impossible for them to express an emotion. The simple task of a father telling a daughter "I love you" can become a monumental accomplishment in a codependent family. For the troubled family, feelings are muted and inexpressible. They feel deep emotions but lack the ability to articulate what they feel. They share rarely.

Such families are also full of compulsive behaviors and compulsive people. Their compulsions serve a purpose. They can best be described as survival behaviors. Even though their compulsions hurt the family in other, more complicated ways, they allow the family to survive. For example, if a father works long and hard at the expense of family relationships, negative feelings can well up inside the children. The children, not knowing how to deal with their emotional deprivation, may eat compulsively in the struggle to survive. But eating is only one of many compulsions cultivated by families in trouble. Drinking, working, stealing, talking, lying, gambling, abusing drugs, and eating are but a few of the compulsions of the codependent.

Compulsions also can serve as a source of protection for the family. As strange as it may seem, the family actually protects the problemed member from being the focus of family pain. For example, if the mother hurts deeply because the father is a workaholic, a son may react by developing a compulsive shoplifting habit. This prevents Dad from being the only villain and diverts some negative feelings away from him. It also enables the son to feel a part of the family system. He gets attention, just like Dad, and feels pain, just like Mom, and in the process has kept Dad from being the sole source of family misery.

In addition to protecting family members from being the source of family pain, another type of compulsive protection occurs in problemed families, that of protecting members from external emotional involvement. An example is the teen-ager from a troubled home who eats compulsively in reaction to her mother's depression. Weight gain becomes a protective barrier from painful emotions in the midst of painful relationships. What appears as self-destruction is really a means of survival. It narrows the individual's world and provides a buffer from potential pain. The paradox in this common family trap is that this form of protection causes greater pain than the avoided poten-

71

tial. The fat teen-ager, in seeking protection, becomes painfully stuck.

Codependency Means Trying Harder

Codependent families are families that try hard. Even when trying hard fails, they try yet harder. They try to resolve the problem, control it, and hide it. Most of all, they try to survive. Not only is personal survival important, but the survival of the family is a major priority. Whether love or anger holds the family together, together is what the individual members are trying to achieve. Trying to survive and keep the family intact is a major obsession with the codependent family.

It becomes obvious to problemed families in the later stages that trying is futile. The trying-hard syndrome only preserves the status quo, prolongs the misery, and prevents long-term recovery from occurring. Eventually, after trying and failing with all the vain attempts at problem resolution, the codependent family must accept that trying harder does not produce results. Trying harder only increases frustration and intensifies family pain.

Codependent families are not aware of what they are doing. They think that in some saintly or dedicated way they are paying a price to revive the family. They believe they are doing what anyone else would do in their situation. This is a major complication in working with members of codependent families. They are so busy acting out roles, reacting to one another, protecting themselves, and trying harder to help that they do not recognize they are codependent. They are active participants in a predictable progression toward disaster. They are too busy to notice that the harder they try to dig out of the family problems, the deeper they sink into codependency.

To recover from codependency, the family needs to recognize (1) they have a problem, (2) they are not unique, and (3) they need outside help.

Recognizing that there is a problem does *not* mean that one person in the family has a problem. It means that the entire family has a problem. The entire family is codependent. The entire family is on a predictable progression away from growth and freedom.

Recognizing that they are not unique means knowing that others have traveled the same path toward destruction, that others have been just as sick and felt just as hopeless.

Recognizing that they need outside help means knowing that continuing to go it alone will only intensify the problem. Hope for the family comes in the form of constructive action in seeking outside help. Problemed families need an objective consultant, a caring and concerned counselor, to assist in untangling the destructive relationships.

Symptoms of the Codependent Family

Codependent families have a lot in common. Some symptoms that crop up in codependent families help us to distinguish between a family that is going through a difficult time and a family that is stuck. A family does not have to have all of the symptoms to be considered codependent. The number of symptoms depends on the longevity of the problem and the stage of the progression. Families in the early stages will have fewer symptoms than those in the late stages.

The following symptoms are not intended to present a depressing picture of the stuck family. They merely assist in the identification of a problem. If we find pictures of our own family within these symptoms, there is cause for hope. Hope comes from taking the proper corrective action once the problem is identified.

1. Deluded by Denial

Stuck families live in a delusional world of denial. They may easily admit that a problem exists, but they deny its intensity or consequences. They suppress an accurate perception of the problem.

Denial also relates to acceptance of responsibility for the problem. Accepting responsibility is not the same as self-blame, which commonly occurs in stuck families. Denial of responsibility relates to the belief either that everything possible has been done or that nothing can be done to make things better.

Denial works in a practical sense like this. A mother has an anorexic daughter. Between the two of them, a "lock up" blocks communication and suppresses emotional expression. The mother might admit that she and her daughter have a problem, but she might fail to realize the problem is potentially fatal if her daughter continues to lose weight. She may write off the entire problem as a phase or a stage that will soon pass. Anorexia nervosa is not just a phase. It destroys a person physically and leaves deep emotional scars. It is no less a problem than cancer. If the mother passes it off as a stage, she is in deep denial of its intensity.

Denial is powerful and difficult to destroy. Many families have continued toward destruction because of deadly denial. The first goal for any stuck family is to break through denial so that recognition and acceptance of the problem can take place.

2. Drowned in a Flood of Negatives

Stuck family members are emotionally deprived. They are saturated and often overwhelmed with the unresolved negative emotions of guilt, anger, and fear. The emotional deprivation that results from these negative feelings eventually engulfs every member of the family.

Guilt. Guilt is both specific and nonspecific. Specific guilt refers to an actual event. Members of stuck families feel specific guilt at times of crisis, wishing that something had been done to prevent another catastrophe. Nonspecific guilt is not tied to a particular event; rather, it is a generalized sense that something is wrong and that someone is to blame. In stuck families, the intensity of specific or nonspecific guilt can increase or decrease, but it is never resolved. Guilt itself is a trap that robs the family of the freedom to feel good. Even though guilt abounds, forgiveness is rare.

Anger. On top of all the guilt is a vast amount of anger. Hostility overflows as each one blames the others for the family's dilemma. Where acceptance exists in other families, stuck families are filled with resentment that often grows into hatred. This high-level personal anger is often manifested in the form of family violence. Stuck families hit each other and wound each other when fits of rage take over.

Fear. Fear is found in large proportion in stuck families. The family members don't trust themselves or one another, so they fear one another. They see their world falling apart, so they fear the world at large. Anxiety is a way of life for the stuck family. They fear that someone will intervene, but they also fear that it will be too late before someone does intervene. Fear, anxiety, and lack of trust are powerful forces that stagnate the family's growth.

Guilt, anger, and fear are just as deadly as denial. They eat away at family relationships and drain family members of their energy. There is nothing fun about living in a family saturated with guilt, anger, and fear. The family and all of life become distorted as a result of this negative saturation.

3. Denial Pregnant with Preoccupation

A paradox in stuck families exists because denial of the problem is accompanied by preoccupation with the problem. At the same time the family is denying the intensity and consequences of the problem, the family is absorbed by it. The family members eat, live, and breathe the problem. They think about it, mull over it, cuss it, and try not to think about it. They are obsessed with covering up the problem and keeping it under control.

Preoccupation with the problem prevents other family members from receiving needed attention. This results in other negative behaviors that result in the neglected family member's receiving attention and recognition, even though it is negative. To the emotionally starved, negative attention is better than no attention at all.

The husband of an alcoholic, while denying the problem, will be preoccupied with it. He will worry about whether or not she is drinking today. When they go out, he will wonder if she will end up drunk. He will try to figure out how to lower her consumption by taking her to safe places, that is, safe places where the wait for dinner is short and the whole process is over quickly. He also will worry about the impact of his wife's drinking on the kids. He will convince himself that they are too young to be affected, at the same time blaming all of the kids' problems on his wife's drinking. He will feel trapped and paralyzed because of the preoccupation. Even if he divorces her, he will remain preoccupied with guilt and will question what might have been if he had handled the problem differently.

4. A Change Without a Change

From time to time the identified problem will stop. The eating stops, the affair is over, the depression lifts, or no more money is gambled away. But even though certain aspects of the stuck family stop, the family does not change.

Even if the gambler stops gambling, nothing has been done to ease the resentment and disappointment from needed money already lost. Accumulated resentment stands in the way of open communication where feelings can be expressed and resolved. Stopping behavior does not initiate recovery because stuck family members are all in it together. Remember the balance we talked about? If one member changes and the rest of the family members stay the same, the family will be out of balance as well as out of joint. If a shift occurs in one family member, a change must occur in all the family members. If one member tries changing alone, a relapse is just around the corner.

So the stuck family stays stuck. The unchanging nature of stuck keeps family members from moving forward while they struggle harder to make things better. But the most likely result is a repeat of the past and more misery from the same source. There's been a change without a change. It's partial at best.

5. Everybody's Out of Control

Another paradox is centered around the concept of control. As time goes on, the family loses more and more control. But as control of the problem lessens, attempts to control everything else intensifies. Parents try to control the children's lives in an effort to spare them. But tight-fisted attempts at control serve only to ignite fires of rebellion within the kids. This propels the family into an even deeper level of being out of control.

A feeling of helplessness results from loss of control. The harder the family tries, the more the family feels like it is holding onto gelatin. The sense of being out of control causes great despair within the family as hopelessness takes over. The harder the family holds on, the more they lose control. The final paradox of control is that *control is gained not from holding on tighter, but from letting go.* Not from preventing consequences, but from letting them happen so that the problemed family member must confront them. Only then is there hope for regaining control. But for stuck families, control is a remote possibility until major changes occur and long-term recovery begins.

6. Inconsistent Behavior

Repeated attempts to control the problem, coupled with the desperation from lack of results, produce inconsistent behaviors that are often in direct opposition to long-established values. In addition, these behaviors are at times antisocial, disruptive, hostile, and aggressive.

Let's see how this works. A very conservative woman may find out that her husband is habitually unfaithful, involved in numerous affairs. Upon her discovery she will most likely feel deeply hurt, and out of a growing depression she will withdraw into herself. She will not want to be around the people who have meant the most to her. Although her friends will notice a change, she will deny that anything is wrong.

As she begins to accept the reality of her marriage, her depression will lift and her anger will emerge. This conservative, quiet female will for the first time in her life become hostile and aggressive, disrupting the family over small issues unrelated to her husband's unfaithfulness.

She may also react by dressing more seductively in an attempt to gain attention from her husband or any other man. She may end up looking and acting exactly opposite from what people expect or are used to. And as she seeks the attention of other men, perhaps becoming involved in an affair herself, she will feel increasingly guilty about her life.

Inconsistent behavior on the part of one mate in reaction to the other mate's problem is common. The children in these families become extremely confused as they model both parents. The inconsistent behavior is found in every family member, which increases the family anxiety and the lack of trust among its members.

Inconsistent behaviors do not remain only within the family interactions. They spread over into work and school. Poor, inconsistent performance at work or school may be the first signal to the outside world that something is wrong in the family. It may also be the loudest cry for help that too often goes unnoticed or ignored.

7. Relationships That Begin to Sputter

Relationships are nearly impossible to sustain in codependent families. The lack of trust and inconsistent and unpredictable behavior eventually take their toll on the relationships between family members. Lies and broken promises drive the individuals away from the family and out into the world in search of a place to belong. Everyone may be struggling to keep the family together and yet at the same time be abandoning the family relationships.

In codependent families the relationships just simply do not work. Mutual give and take does not happen. Roles are established whereby a person is either a giver or a taker. The givers eventually burn out, and the takers are never satisfied. Eventually even sick relationships are replaced by rigid roles. Individuals play out the roles alongside other family members, not in relation to them. The fulfillment of each role in the struggle to survive becomes the priority for each person. In this survival scheme, relationships break down, stagnate, and die.

8. Moods on a Swinging Pendulum

Extreme mood swings are prevalent in the members of families in trouble. Each member can be found vacillating between levels of depression and manic euphoria. Facial expressions vary from flattened, dull affect to childlike anticipation.

The depression is often caused by emotional deprivation and loss of expectations. Thus, when new expectations arise such as, "This time is the last time Daddy will ever gamble," the depression lifts, hope is restored, and the family is almost in a state of euphoria. Before long, however, the honeymoon is over, and hopes are dashed with more unfulfilled promises. In the later stages, when hope is completely gone, the manic euphoria returns no more. The moods swing between deep depression and a dull numbness. Whatever the mood, stuck families are insured that it will not last long. Inconsistency becomes the rule when it comes to emotions.

9. Facts That Are Closer to Fiction

A lot of lying and deception are necessary in codependent families. Problemed families feel they must hide the problem from themselves and the rest of the world. A unique characteristic of codependent families is that they place great value in misleading information if it is more comfortable or more acceptable than the truth.

A child in a codependent family learns that if Dad abandons the family for his office, if he is caught up in workaholism to the extent that everyone around him is miserable, the problem can neatly be described as "strong ambition." Codependent families call fat children "big boned." They call depressed people "loners." And they call heavy drinkers "people that really enjoy their drinking." After a while, this distorted way of looking at their world becomes a habit. Reality is replaced immediately with a more palatable mirage of normalcy. So if you ask a codependent family member to tell you what is happening, chances are that the report will not be accurate.

The problem is compounded by the family's inclination toward grandiosity, which becomes a form of compensation to fill the voids that exist. Grandiose people tell you what they hope will happen, not what will probably happen. And they tell you a possibility as if it is already a reality. Grandiose people lie because they feel inadequate. Truth is not enough to satisfy their emptiness. So the codependent family is a most unreliable source of information, especially when the truth interferes with the struggle to survive.

10. Judgmental Attitude Toward Others

Out of a sense of inferiority, codependent family members become judgmental. *Hypercritical* is perhaps a better word to describe how they view one another and the rest of the world. To them, no one can do things better, no one is good enough, and everyone fails to measure up to their expectations.

From this judgmental attitude comes a perfectionism that focuses on performance. Emphasis is shifted from who people are and how they relate to what they are doing. Becoming and relating give way to the importance of achieving. But achieving is never enough, and it is judged inadequate.

A perfectionistic brother may feel driven to run for class president. His sister is supportive of the venture. But her judgmental mind set will ensure a defeat, whether he wins or loses. If he does not win, she will chastise him for not working hard enough to secure the victory. If he does win, she will write off the significance of the win with statements concerning the weakness of the opponent. Although this example is simplistic, it demonstrates the trap that develops when a family is both judgmental and perfectionistic. Individuals always strive to achieve the best but are always judged less than best.

These same principles apply even more when the codependent family sizes up those outside the family. Their critical perspective demoralizes other people and organizations. Their negativity affects everyone around them. Their negative, judgmental, and perfectionist attitude serves to distance the codependent family from the rest of the world.

11. Illness After Illness

All of the symptoms discussed here work together to place a tremendous amount of stress on the codependent family. This stress eventually takes a physical toll on family members. Ulcers, colds, allergies, hypertension, headaches, backaches, and intestinal problems are common in the codependent family. These illnesses require treatment and attention.

Yet, these illnesses may be a form of compensation for family problems because the treatment of the illnesses diverts treatment from the real problem. If the family is busy treating the obvious, it may be too busy to discover the need for treating the emotional problem hidden below the physical one. In addition, by treating the physical illness the codependent family members may deceive themselves into feeling progress is being made.

These illnesses don't just happen. We now know that a number of common physical problems (such as high blood pressure and ulcers) come from our own internal stress. Stress-related diseases indicate that something is gravely wrong and in need of treatment. It is amazing how many families lower their medical bills after they take the needed steps to get unstuck.

If It's Not One Thing, It's Another

The compilation of all the symptoms produces a group of struggling people who will eventually have problems in every area of their lives.

- **Mental Problems.** Difficulty concentrating, memory problems and loss, inability to think clearly.

- **Emotional Problems.** Mood swings, depression, inability to identify and express emotions, constant feelings of discomfort.

- **Social Problems.** Surface relationships, feeling alien and distant from others, reclusive and reserved.

- **Physical Problems.** Chronic illnesses, lack of energy, weight gain or loss.

- **Spiritual Problems.** Alienation from God, constant sense that something is missing, lack of direction for growth.

As problems progress, complications increase for the co-dependent family. The symptoms become more obvious and harder to deny in the later stages. It is important to remember that the progression can end at any time. When the family identifies that it is codependent and accepts responsibility to take action, it can move out of codependency and into recovery. Recovery is always an option for the codependent family.

The Progressive Stages
of the Codependent Family

The family was confused. Something was not right. Lisa, mother of three, was different from the person she used to be. She had never stopped taking the mild tranquilizer prescribed by her physician when her twin sister died. Robert, her husband, had discussed the problem with Lisa repeatedly. He would tell her that the children were concerned and that they felt something was wrong. For a few days she would appear to be normal, but it never lasted. The family distrusted their feelings that she needed help. They wanted to believe her demands that she was simply under a lot of stress.

The situation got worse. Lisa had difficulty getting up in the mornings, would return to bed in the afternoon and would go to bed early at night. Her pill consumption increased as her ability to relate to the family decreased. Robert finally refused to talk about the problem with the girls. Everybody felt terrible about the problem, but no one talked about it anymore. Eventually, Robert stopped seeing his friends and turned down all invitations to go anywhere. The girls no longer invited their friends to the house. The family covered up what could not be denied: the mother was addicted to tranquilizers.

Robert tried to control the problem. He started going home for lunch. He hired a housekeeper. He arranged for the two of them to get away frequently on weekends. When he found any pills, he would flush them down the toilet, only to find that more had been hidden in other places. Nothing worked. The more he tried to control the problem the worse the problem became.

Robert questioned his own sanity. He felt paralyzed. His daughters, wanting no part of their mother or father, spent as little time at home as possible. Finally, Lisa took a handful of tranquilizers and sleeping pills and was near death when Robert found her. He rushed her to the hospital where her stomach was pumped and she was nursed back to health. At least temporarily.

Months went by. Lisa continued to live in a daze of drugged awareness, and Robert felt deserted and lonely. He decided his marriage was over, and he began to date a woman he had met at work. He was going to divorce Lisa. He sent Lisa to live with her mother and father, and he began to start his life on a new course. The two daughters felt themselves to be helpless and their mom hopeless. They were hurt and disgusted by it all.

Robert and his daughters began to compensate for the problem. The oldest daughter was driven to achieve more and more. Anything less than perfection was unacceptable. Her sister was just the opposite. She began to fail miserably as she spent more and more time with her friends. Her friends were involved in drugs and were anything but healthy. Robert busied himself developing a new look for himself. He bought new clothes and a new car to promote his new image. Everyone compensated for the guilt and anger felt over the situation with Lisa.

But no matter what they did, they could not lessen the impact of Lisa's wasted life on their own lives. Each one might survive, including Lisa, but they would all remain affected until each person received help and treatment.

Robert, Lisa, and their two daughters were typical of a co-dependent family. Codependent families are on a predictable progression toward disaster. The path can be chronicled through six stages. Although identified as distinct phases, in real life the stages are not so clear cut. Families flow from one to another and, at any given time, could simultaneously experience aspects of two different stages. We divide the progression into these stages in order to assist in the identification process.

Frequently when this material has been presented to a co-dependent family member, he or she has been able to point out the stage in which the family functions. The person who was in denial has been able to accept help because of the identification with a particular stage. It is also common to have someone say that the family is living in a combination of the stages, that there are behaviors from stages one through six. In any case, the importance lies in the ability to identify some level of codependency and start to move out of it.

There is a seventh stage—the stage of creation and recovery. It is the time when the family begins again, when it moves out of established roles and into the recovery process. Any family can move from stage one or two or three to stage seven at any time. All that is necessary is the willingness to do whatever it takes.

Stage One: Confusion
("Is There a Problem or Isn't There")

At the first stage, there is a growing awareness that something is not right about the family. Each member begins to realize that there is a problem that is not getting better. This awareness often is a result of embarrassment or humiliation by the person with the identified problem.

When the gambler goes on a gambling spree and overdraws all the checking accounts, the embarrassment comes when the bank calls. More embarrassment and humiliation are added when checks bounce and stores call to request their money. When the kids must do without necessities because Dad has blown all of the money, humiliation does not quite describe the feeling.

Long discussions between the gambler and spouse will begin. And after all of the discussing is over, promises for change will be made. The promises will signify the ability to control the problem. And in this first stage, the person will be able to control the problem. But the ability to control a problem does not lessen its intensity. A problem is a problem whether it can be controlled or not.

In the case of the gambler, he will not return to the tables for some time. The calls to the bookies will stop, and he will prove to himself and the family that the problem is under control.

The family had feared the father would not stop gambling

and that all the money would be wasted away. Then the gambler stopped gambling. He appears to have no problem in controlling the urge to make a bet. So, the family is greatly *confused*.

In the times of abstinence and restraint, family members are led to believe that they have overreacted. When everything is functioning normally, they feel that they not only have overreacted but also have been disloyal. These feelings are enhanced by the gambler's not gambling and by his acting out the role of perfect husband and father. Flowers for Mom and time with the kids cause them to feel guilty because they had been thinking that Dad was out of control. The confusion over who is the real Dad and what is the real problem strains all of the family relations. The kids doubt themselves, and they doubt their mother's judgment and wonder whether she is the problem instead of Dad.

As the confusion continues, different family members ask questions and seek advice from relatives and friends. Convinced that the problem is manageable and in control, they have little fear in discussing the issue. After all, the problem is controllable. The confusion gets worse when advice from different sources isn't in agreement. One friend may say that all is well and congratulate the family on the ability to bring the problem under control. Another friend may suggest professional help, saying that temporary control is no indication of long-term recovery. That friend will confuse the family but will also be stating the difficult truth the family needs to hear. It is only a matter of time until the problem returns.

Whether it is gambling, as in the example above, or one of hundreds of other problems, temporary times when the problem is under control have nothing to do with the recovery. An alcoholic who stops drinking periodically is still an alcoholic. A rapist who has not attacked for a month is still a rapist. The times of control only serve to confuse the family even more. The family is torn between a feeling of progress and a feeling of impending doom.

Stage Two: Cover-Up ("Let's Not Talk About It")

The inevitable happens. The untreated alcoholic drinks again, the gambler gambles, and on it goes. The family realizes that the problem is more severe than they had imagined. They construct a wall between them and the world to hide the problem and to *cover up* the evidence. Other walls are constructed to keep the problem from one another. Family members begin to live in a delusional world of denial and lies.

Rationalization—explaining away the real reasons in order to justify attitude or behavior—is a key component in the cover-up between family members. They rationalize that everyone has problems. They convince themselves that their problem is only a phase or a stage due to outside pressure. They try to assess blame and avoid responsibility. They rationalize that nothing can be done and yet try everything possible to hide the problem.

One of the strongest family rules begins to surface in this stage. It is the rule, "Don't talk about the problem." Topics surrounding the problem are avoided. No one expresses an opinion, no one is allowed to share feelings about the situation. If anyone dares to bring up or hint at the issue, silence and stares of disapproval serve as power restraints.

The outside world is approached in much the same way. The issue is avoided with other people. "Loving" friends help veer the conversation in opposite directions from the issue. If the problem is mentioned, its severity is minimized. If outright lying to friends is needed to uphold the family reputation, then lying will be used.

The family of the overeater will talk of the weight problem as past tense. They will relate, "Of course there was a problem, but have you seen Billie lately? The new diet is really working . . . ," even if Billie has gained twenty pounds in the past month.

The alcoholic family may admit that drinking was a problem, but they will tell of a marvelous change. They may relate how seldom Mom or Dad or the husband or wife ever drinks, even if only the night before there was another incident of uncontrollable drunkenness.

Denial and minimization become major obsessions with the

family. They become willing to do whatever it takes to cover up the intensity of the problem. This means that the family must eventually close up into itself. Exposure to the outside world has to be lessened. Social engagements must be turned down. Events where identification of the problem could happen must be avoided. The goal is to create the perfect family illusion. And for that to happen, everyone must be an active participant. But as the family discovers, the ability to cover up the problem is only temporary. When the problem can no longer be denied or minimized, the family slips into the third stage.

Stage Three: Control ("We Can Handle It Ourselves")

When the problem can no longer be covered up, the focus shifts to controlling the problem. Since great effort went into covering up the problem and that effort proved futile, the family desperately attempts to *control* the problem. The symptoms have become undeniable, and the problem is obvious to anyone close to the family. As the problem grows greater, the family increases its efforts to bring the problem under control.

The stage of control could also accurately be named, "The Search for Home Remedies." Each person does everything in his or her power to bring the problem under control. And at times there are some short intervals of control. But they are temporary. Just when the family feels it has found the answer, the home remedy proves ineffective in producing long-term results.

The family attempts at control are quite varied. A wife may seek new friends for a husband. Parents may move in order to get their child or children into a different school. Or a move of greater distance (called a geographical cure) may occur in an attempt to heal the entire family. Dogs, cats, faith healers, wood working tools, recipe books, hobbies of all types, night school, or positive thinking cassette tapes may all be used in an attempt to bring some relief from the problem.

Even longer discussions will occur between the spouses in a search for the cause of the problem. Pleas for change and promises to do better happen more frequently. But the discussions often heat up into yelling and screaming matches. Verbal confrontation often becomes physical as spouses become more frustrated over the inability to help.

Family members become consumed with guilt, shame, and remorse. They feel guilty over not being able to correct the problem. They feel shame from living in a failing family. And they feel remorse over all of the destruction from the past. The individuals hurt deeply for themselves and for the person they are trying to control.

Because all-out attempts to control have been made, and because all of the attempts have proved futile, family members feel inadequate and inferior. This sense of inadequacy causes more compensating behaviors outside the family. The struggle to survive becomes a difficult, complicated progression of behaviors that produce still more frustration and even less relief. The family trying to control the problem is hurt and exhausted. It is also a collection of disappointed people as the expectations of normal family life disappear and expectations of more difficulty rise.

Stage Four: Chaos ("What Do We Do Now")

The *chaos* stage is the most traumatic. It is full of indecision and lack of direction. In attempting to cover up and control the problem, the family had a common goal. Everyone was involved in the same mission. But when the problem gets out of control, the family is shattered. Full of fear and anxiety over what is happening, the family doesn't know what to do next.

Chaos identifies a family out of control. Problems multiply and solutions seem remote. The family can no longer hide its dysfunction. Fraught with problems, the family is in crisis.

Because so much effort has been futile, the family is paralyzed in its misery. Family members are afraid to act. At the same time, they are afraid of not acting in time. They are haunted by the fear that someone may die or be hurt irreparably. Paradoxically, family violence is common in this stage.

Family members feel that they are crazy. They question every interaction, every statement. They attempt to discover evidence of their own insanity. They feel unique, that they are traveling in uncharted territory where no one has been before. They believe that few could understand their situation and that even fewer would want to.

The family's entire world is affected by this chaos. The kids do poorly in school, and the parents do poorly at work. Relationships within and without the family are destroyed. Communication becomes a monumental task. The family feels and, to outsiders, looks hopeless.

Even in chaos the family, through habit, continues its fruitless attempts to cover up the magnitude of their problem for outsiders. But the attempts of family members to hide the problems from one another stop because they have no more energy to support the delusion. The only thing the family can manage to cover up now is its ability to solve the problem and re-create the family. Ultimately, the individuals convince themselves that the ability to take constructive action is gone.

In the stage of chaos, crisis is a frequent event: a legal crisis, because a family member ends up in jail; a medical crisis, because of drugs, drinking, eating, not eating, or family violence; an economic crisis, because a job is lost or money is wasted; a social crisis, because the family is no longer welcome at social gatherings and the family no longer has any interest in being with others. Crisis after crisis will hit the family. Big and little, these crises will sustain the high level of chaos within the family.

Trust is absent at this stage. No one has made the situation better. No one has relieved the pain. Promises have turned to lies. False hopes have faded into helplessness. In chaos, family members are full of self-pity as they assess their dilemma and compare their family to others. Pain, indirection, and fear become unbearable. Eventually the members of the family want out.

Stage Five: Cancellation
("Someone's Got to Go, and It's Not Me")

In the *cancellation* stage, the problem is considered to be permanent and beyond hope. The family's journey through helplessness has left it with the belief that the person with the problem is unchangeable. As these beliefs and thoughts crystallize, the family begins the process of dissociation from the problem. This dissociation process eventually ends in various forms of cancellation, or physical separation. But whatever the form, the emotional turmoil will keep each person chained to the problem.

The family goes through a stage of being torn between staying with the problem or getting away from it. But as the cancellation stage solidifies, family members utilize various forms of separation. Some families eventually use all these means of separation and cancellation to distance themselves from the problem. And as they are used, the family does stabilize. It moves from chaos into a more focused direction. This stability is falsely perceived by the family as progress.

The first form of cancellation occurs while all of the family members are still around. It is a process of literally *depersonalizing* the person with a problem. Rather than view the drug-addicted teen-ager as a human being, they instead view the child as a problem. They begin talking about the problem rather than the person. Sometimes a dad who is greatly disappointed in his son will refuse to talk to the boy or to acknowledge his presence. Frequently the individual, still living in the home, is treated like a piece of furniture, ignored and abandoned. As far as the family is concerned, the problemed person has no role and no responsibilities.

Another form of cancellation is *physical separation*. In this form, the person is moved out of the home. Treatment for the person may be sought, not with the belief that he or she will get well, but with the desire to get the person away from them for a while. Frequently families will force someone into treatment and then never participate in the process. They have a you-fix-it attitude. The treatment may even be viewed as a source of punishment.

There are other means of temporary cancellation. Parents send kids off to academies. A spouse may seek a job where extended travel is the norm. If teen-agers hold out long enough, they can make it to a college in a distant town. Summer camps and separate vacations are also sources of short-term separation from the problemed person.

Longer-term cancellation also comes in a variety of forms. The most common when the husband or wife has the problem is divorce. This divorce may be legal, but it is rarely final. It is amazing to see the husbands and wives still locked into unhealthy relationships with each other long after the divorce is over. The continued emotional hookups and the dependency that is frequently fostered are results of guilt and irresponsibility. This form of cancellation is rarely effective in getting unhooked from the person with the problem. Legal separation has little influence on the emotions, as will be presented in the following stage.

There are other ways of cancelling the relationships within the family. Young girls get pregnant and marry young. Young boys get girls pregnant and marry young. Kids get into legal trouble and wind up in juvenile hall or jail for a long time. Cancellation and separation come in many forms for the kids and parents in problemed families. But when cancellation happens, the emptiness left must be filled in some way.

Stage Six: Compensation
("Let's Get Busy, So We Don't Have to Deal with It")

After the cancellation of relationships occurs, the family is left with an overabundance of unresolved emotions. Feelings of guilt over the decision to separate eat away at the ability to recover. Accompanying the guilt are bitter anger and resentment toward the other person and resentment at the destruction that has ensued over the years. Complicating the emotional swamp is the occasional reminder of the good times from the past. Often the emotional turmoil plunges the person into a quagmire of depression. Loneliness and isolation are characteristic of the beginnings of the compensation stage. All of these elements combine to produce the emptiness that drives a person to compensate.

Inaction and procrastination earmark the compensation stage. After years of trying hard, the individual, tired and emotionally exhausted, finds difficulty getting into action again. In the search for a way to energize, the individual withdraws from friends and family. This state of isolation is only temporary, however. The person eventually emerges with an aggressive surge to recapture the good times and good feelings lost in the past.

What appears to be a family in recovery is actually a group of people involved in some type of diversionary activity. This activity keeps them from having to deal with the real issues gripping them. They are driven to do something that will prevent looking back. Some members get caught up in a new career; some go back to school to meet people or to gain a new skill. These activities may appear appropriate, but they are not going to lead to recovery. Becoming involved in civic organizations or holding offices in clubs is a change from isolation, but, again, this is diversion. Working hard and obtaining promotions also looks positive, but this too is a detour from the recovery process.

When the individual gets caught up in activities that look positive and productive, resolution of the past is delayed. The past continues to creep into the present. Often the person seeking escape repeats the past. An excellent example of this is the frequency with which husbands and wives remarry alcoholics. Less obvious is the wife of an alcoholic who marries a workaholic and experiences once again a less than adequate relationship.

Why do so many repeat the past? One theory is that it is a compensatory effort to cure a second or third person, any person, since the individual was unable to cure the first mate. The emptiness from not helping the first mate is unresolved and the individual tries to relieve this unfinished business by helping someone else. It is an unconscious effort to prove that the individual really was not the cause of the first mate's problem.

The problem is paralleled by the children in the family. A girl in the family of a workaholic may marry a workaholic. She finds herself in exactly the situation she hated while growing up. Without help for the affected children, these experiences are common.

Another theory about why people repeat the past has to do with survival roles. If a person is stuck in the role of enabler, he or she unconsciously will be attracted to another person with a problem. If an individual knows only enabling behaviors, then the individual will find a relationship in which those enabling behaviors can be utilized. It is the ultimate form of codependency with tragedy waiting to be repeated.

Compensation is common after cancellation. It comes in many forms. But whether it is in the form of intellectualism or religious fanaticism, it only serves to delay recovery. And what about the family members who had the original problem? Where is the hope for recovery for the person who has been rejected and often depersonalized?

Remaining codependent is so unnecessary and a tremendous waste of lives. The entire progression through the stages is needless, and it *can be diverted at any time*. When the family becomes willing to do whatever it takes, it can move from any stage directly into the final stage of creation and recovery. A new family can be created, and everyone in the family can recover hope and health.

Stage Seven: Creation ("Rome Wasn't Built in a Day— Neither Are Healthy Families")

Moving out of the six progressive stages and into the *creation* and *recovery* of a healthy family is a complicated endeavor. What has taken years to develop cannot be undone in a day, a month, or a year. It is a long process, yet compared to the progression of the problem, it is an easy solution. But the family must be willing to expend as much energy in resolving its problems as it took in maintaining them.

One difficulty with initiating recovery is that not everyone is at the same point of desperation or readiness for help. While one is ready to seek help, the others may still be in a strong state of denial. This should not discourage the ready family member from taking action. When one person moves out and accepts responsibility to help the situation, the others usually follow.

The first step in moving from codependency to recovery is reaching out for professional help, and that professional should be a specialist with experience in the area of the problem. If someone buys a new Chevrolet and problems arise with the engine, most people would take it to a shop that has worked on a lot of

Chevrolets. The same principle should apply for families. Families have wasted thousands of dollars on treatment undertaken by people who are simply incompetent in some areas.

When seeking help for an eating problem in the family, the family must be sure the professional has worked with people with eating disorders, not just read about them or heard lectures on them. Alcoholics need treatment from people who know the principles of long-term sobriety. A counselor who only helps the alcoholic figure out *why* the drinking started and doesn't help the alcoholic *stop* drinking and start living is not helping the alcoholic. If that same counselor works with the family, most likely that counselor would not be of much help.

Treatment of the family varies according to the nature of the problem and the devastation experienced by the family. It also has a lot to do with the person identified as having the original problem. One common mistake made by families is to wait for the person with the original problem to be ready and willing before seeking help. This should never happen. The very act of the rest of the family seeking help greatly increases the chances for recovery and reduces the time the person must suffer.

Treatment is an ongoing process that must involve the entire family. It should never be viewed as a cure or a one-time event. It is a time when everyone in the family learns to develop the art of helpful interaction instead of the destructive habit of enabling. This increases the chances of recovery for the person with the identified problem and for everyone else in the family. The ability to be helpful rather than enabling takes time and effort to learn.

In treatment, problems are dealt with and discussed openly. What is done in the presence of the counselor serves as practice for times later when the counselor is not present. What had been covered up or minimized is presented realistically and handled carefully. Members are able to express their feelings in relation to reality rather than cover up and suppress emotions. Each individual is able to deal with his or her own guilt, fear, and anger. The resolution of these feelings is essential for recovery and for preventing the past from being repeated.

When the whole family enters treatment, the ability to trust and forgive one another returns. Trust and forgiveness take time to achieve. But when all are making an attempt, both trust and forgiveness come much easier. As trust develops, family members are able to resume their responsibilities. They also can break out of the established roles of survival and experience the freedom of relationships developing rather than roles being maintained.

Treatment is also a time for resolving lost expectations. If a father of an anorexic teen-ager has missed the fun of watching his daughter bloom through adolescence, he must deal with and accept the loss. If an adolescent teen-ager has missed her father's involvement while growing up, because of his compulsive workaholism, she must rid herself of resentment.

Treatment helps the family establish realistic family and personal goals. Too often people expect too much too soon. The first months of recovery can be filled with bitter disappointment. Treatment reveals what can be anticipated realistically in the first months. Then short-term and long-term goals can be established to promote growth rather than destroy it.

The possibility of relapse is always an area covered in treatment. Although not wanting to admit it, everyone is afraid of relapse. Once it is discussed, the pressure of possible relapse is relieved. The family is even able to make plans if it does happen.

Treatment begins the recovery process. Recovery is the creation of a new family, a family that is supportive of one another. It is the creation of a family based in reality and able to handle problems constructively. It is not the creation of a family without problems. It is the creation of a family who recognizes that problems do not destroy, they help the family grow and mature.

Freedom to Make Choices

The recovery process creates a family that is free to make choices—the exact opposite of being trapped in a progression toward disaster. The family in recovery has alternatives that were not available before. Ten options represent the creation of a new family through recovery.

1. No longer running from problems. Facing problems with wisdom.
2. Not looking for reasons why or for someone to blame. Searching for answers and solutions.
3. Not waiting for the person with the original problem to take action or make a decision. Taking action and making decisions for change regardless of the desires of others.
4. Not attempting to control the problems. Assisting in the resolution of the problem.
5. No longer making futile threats. Saying what is meant and doing what is said.
6. No longer accepting or extracting promises. Supporting positive action for change.
7. No longer seeking advice from the uninformed. Seeking help from professionals with experience in the problem.
8. No longer nagging, preaching, coaxing, or lecturing. Utilizing factual, nonjudgmental reporting of inappropriate behavior to keep the family rooted in reality.
9. Not allowing family violence. Handling problems in a constructive manner that brings resolution before violence erupts.
10. No longer feeling alone or crazy. Recovering with supportive people who care, people who have been through the same problems, realizing that without them, long-term recovery is not possible.

Start moving toward recovery!

It's "Just a Phase"

"Oh, you know, Jack's forty-five now. Some men have to go through phases like that."

Maybe you know this man or his family. What about the following example? Does it sound familiar?

"Cathy *has* lost a lot of weight, but I'm not worried about it. She used to be a little on the heavy side, and the kids used to tease her at school. But now her hormones are changing. She's a little underweight, but it's just a phase. She'll start eating again soon."

Let's look at a few families and individuals going through a "phase."

Six Problems in Seven Stages

The following section tracks some specific problems through the six stages of the progressing problem and the seventh stage of creation and recovery. For each problem an example of a behavior is listed for each stage to demonstrate how the progression may happen.

1. Sex. Problem: A father and husband is involved in an affair with another woman

Stage One: Confusion. The wife cannot explain the increasing absences from home and the increasing number of hang-up phone calls. The two discuss that, once again, something is going on. The husband admits someone has been after him. He promises to take care of it. She feels that she has overreacted.

Stage Two: Cover-Up. Both husband and wife start to lie to the children about the problem. The two no longer talk to each other about the possibility of another woman. They stop going to parties together. When they do, they act as if they are greatly infatuated with each other. They attempt to make everyone believe all is well.

Stage Three: Control. The wife attempts to find some more interesting friends, having separated herself from her old friends. She hopes these friends and their husbands will motivate her husband to change. She continues to find evidence that the affair continues, such as lipstick on a collar and the scent of a strange perfume. She screams, yells, and pleads for him to stop. Feeling inadequate, she seeks attention from other men, finally becoming involved in her own affair.

Stage Four: Chaos. The wife finally catches her husband with the other woman in public. She realizes that separation is inevitable. To endear her children to herself, she allows them to do what they want and stops all disciplining. The children are confused, not knowing whether to side with their mother or father. They realize the family is going to change and fear what that could mean. The mother quits her part-time job and finds a full-time job in anticipation of living without her husband.

Stage Five: Cancellation. The wife accepts her husband as terminally insecure and unable to function without affection outside of the marriage. She convinces herself that the situation is hopeless. One day her husband comes home to find that she and the children have moved across town. He pleads for them to return, promising eternal faithfulness. The children are still torn between the two parents. They are angry with the father but feel guilty for leaving him. The support of two households produces financial problems. Everyone feels victimized and trapped.

Stage Six: Compensation. The wife changes jobs again and becomes immersed in her career. One of the daughters becomes promiscuous in an unconscious attempt to obtain the attention of her father or his replacement. Other compensating behaviors are found in the children, such as attempts at super-achievement in school accompanied by great frustration at never being able to achieve enough. The wife falls in love with a compulsive workaholic from her place of employment. The children realize they are in for a whole new set of difficulties.

Stage Seven: Creation and Recovery. Rather than separate, the husband and wife agree to go for marriage counseling. The counselor suggests that the husband spend the next six months in a recovery house close to home. This will provide an opportunity for communication and role clarification with less day-to-day pressure. The husband and wife go for counseling together twice a week, and they are joined by the children once a week for family therapy. After six months, the father moves back home. The whole family follows up with weekly participation at a recovery group. The family learns to trust one another and finds forgiveness of the past.

2. Drugs. Problem: A teen-ager in the family is involved with marijuana and other street drugs

Stage One: Confusion. The boy's mother finds some strange paraphernalia in his room. He accuses her of invading his privacy. He convinces her that he took it away from a friend in an attempt to save his life. The mother feels terrible over the incident and questions her effectiveness as a mother.

Stage Two: Cover-Up. The topic of drugs is not discussed by the mother. She decides not to tell her husband that her suspicions continue. The other brothers and sisters are aware of the problem, but if they mention the topic, they are told to shut up. When the school calls to question the boy's increasing absences from school in the afternoon, the mother apologizes and explains that the boy suffers from low blood sugar. She agrees to talk to her son. When she does talk to him, he cries and talks about being very depressed. He agrees to see a counselor for his bad moods. The mother feels relief.

Stage Three: Control. The mother is awakened at 3:00 A.M. to find that some kids dumped her son onto the front lawn strung out and out of control. In fear she rushes him to an emergency room. The next day the father takes away the car and grounds him for three months. All phone calls are intercepted. The parents vacillate between pleading for change and punishing the boy. Yelling and screaming are interrupted by times of isolating and ignoring the son. The parents feel like failures, but they are determined to keep a tight lid on the problem.

Stage Four: Chaos. The boy ends up with a case of infectious hepatitis. The physician tells the parents it is from a dirty needle. The tension between the parents increases. They find it difficult to talk to each other. The wife blames the husband, and the husband blames the wife. Neither knows what to do. The father begins to "ride herd" on the other children. His disciplinary grip tightens in an attempt to save the other kids from drugs. The kids rebel and start to separate emotionally from the family.

Stage Five: Cancellation. The problem continues, but to avoid any violence within the family, the drug-addicted son is ignored whenever possible. Finally, in desperation the parents kick the boy out without offering him any alternatives for treatment.

Stage Six: Compensation. The parents feel great depression over their son and their handling of the problem. They are angry at themselves and everyone else. They are extremely hard on the other children, trying to make them compensate for the loss of their brother. The father works later and later, while the mother spends more and more time away from home. The family functions in a painful daze, wishing things were different and staying very busy in a struggle not to think about the missing son.

Stage Seven: Creation and Recovery. Rather than kick the boy out, the family offers alternatives. One of those alternatives is treatment. The other individuals begin receiving treatment long before the boy is willing to accept help. Eventually they are all involved in treatment in which they learn to live differently. They all accept responsibility to work on themselves. Slowly, relationships are strengthened and each person begins to set priorities that are appropriate. Everyone stays involved in some type of recovery and support group. Each member begins to let go of the trivial and to develop a spiritual perspective from which to view life and to undertake achievements.

3. Alcohol. Problem: An alcoholic wife and mother continues
to drink uncontrollably time after time

Stage One: Confusion. The wife becomes intoxicated at a couple of parties but explains that she has been taking a new medication causing the extreme reaction to the alcohol. She promises that it won't happen again. The husband is worried and confused, but he does not press the issue any further.

Stage Two: Cover-Up. As the drinking continues, so does the rationalization. She pleads that her body is changing, that her problem with alcohol is only temporary. The husband begins to turn down invitations, explaining that his health is failing. He makes excuses to the children and refuses to talk about the problem.

Stage Three: Control. The husband can no longer cover up the problem. He pours out all of the alcohol in an attempt to control the problem. He takes over the checkbook, limiting the money she has to spend. He destroys her credit cards trying to totally remove any possibility of her purchasing alcohol. He sends the kids away to camp, hoping that it will lessen the pressure and decrease her need to drink. Out of frustration, he takes an if-you-can't-beat-'em-join-'em attitude, and he starts to drink.

Stage Four: Chaos. The drinking worsens. The husband is afraid she will kill herself or someone else. The kids are disgusted with Mom and cannot understand Dad's inability to help the situation. They each feel some responsibility for the problem. The husband does not know where to turn. He feels helpless and crazy. He questions whether or not he is the cause of the family turmoil.

Stage Five: Cancellation. After all attempts to control the problem, the husband divorces the alcoholic wife. The children sink into a deep depression over the family being torn apart.

Stage Six: Compensation. Soon after the divorce the husband marries a woman half his age. He demands her total dependency upon him. His feelings of impotence to change his first wife are countered with total dominance over the second. The children resent the new wife and lose all respect for their father. Each one moves away from the father and mother as soon as possible. Distant colleges and jobs out of state eventually provide the excuses to leave. But each child's life is not his or her own. It is a reaction to the past. The past will leave its imprint on each life.

Stage Seven: Creation and Recovery. The entire family goes through treatment with the mother. Alcoholics Anonymous, Alanon, Aftercare, family therapy, and recovery support groups are all part of creating a new family. It is not long before each member has broken out of his or her survival role and started to relate to the others in a new way. They are even able to develop a sense of gratitude for the opportunity to start over. Expressions of care, concern, and love are openly initiated by everyone in the family.

4. Food. Problem: A daughter develops anorexia nervosa and must struggle to stay alive

Stage One: Confusion. The daughter begins to lose a lot of weight, her eating is inconsistent, and her mood is depressed. When questioned about the problem, she insists that she is only getting ready for summer. She says she wants to look like the girls in the ads when swimsuit weather hits. The mother is worried, but she accepts it as a valid reason for dieting.

Stage Two: Cover-Up. The mother provides the money for a complete wardrobe change. She assists her daughter in buying bulky clothes to disguise the weight loss that continues. Everyone passes it off as a stage and would never admit that the girl has an eating disorder in need of treatment. Her brother and sister worry about her, but they never mention her weight. The father pleads with the mother to do something.

Stage Three: Control. The parents take direct action. They begin to bribe her to eat. Promises of cars and horses motivate public gorging followed by secret vomiting. The parents try to spend more time with her, and the more time they spend, the less she eats. Threats of institutionalization produce only short-term weight gain. Neither hobbies nor horses are enough to reverse the disorder.

Stage Four: Chaos. The entire focus of family attention is on the girl. Every action is a reaction to her problem. Her weight drops to eighty-seven pounds. Everyone is afraid she will not get better. Her brother and sister express their anger and rage at the parents' inability to help their sister. They find different activities that ensure less time spent at home. One day when the girl passes out, the parents take her to an emergency room. The physician informs the parents that she is near death and admits her to the hospital for treatment. The parents fight frequently and separate often. The brother and sister fear for the security of their lives.

Stage Five: Cancellation. While in the hospital the anorexic girl gains weight gradually. While she is away, the family starts to regroup without her. Plans are made for her to enter a long-term home for intensive psychiatric treatment. The family rarely discusses her or her condition.

Stage Six: Compensation. The whole family struggles for normality, but emptiness prevails. The brother becomes heavily involved in drugs in an attempt to escape. The sister gains fifty pounds in six months. The father spends more time than ever before away from the family playing golf and tennis whenever possible. The mother, greatly grieved, seeks psychiatric help for her depression. She is put on antidepressant drugs.

Stage Seven: Creation and Recovery. The daughter, in addition to receiving medical care, enters into an eating disorder treatment program in which the entire family is involved. Rather than drugs, the brother gets involved with a youth group at the church nearby. The husband and wife free each other from blame and support each other through the trauma. The sister has no need to eat excessively. The focus of the family is no longer on the eating disorder. The girl with the eating disorder develops a new concept of herself. She begins to grow personally and in the relationship of her family. Slowly she feels the freedom of loving her parents return.

5. Gambling. Problem: A man moves from gambling for fun to a compulsive habit that consumes his life and that of his family

Stage One: Confusion. The wife is confused by an increase in out-of-town trips without her. She finds money from checking accounts and savings accounts mysteriously missing. She confronts her husband, and he explains that he invested some money for their retirement and lost it. He explains the trips are a means of getting back the money. She remains suspicious but accepts the excuse as truth.

Stage Two: Cover-Up. The husband changes jobs because he knows that his performance is lagging and that management is about to take action. The wife lies to her friends about her husband's problem and about why they are so badly in debt. When in public she praises him as a hard worker and good provider. The wife takes a job to help the family get out of debt.

Stage Three: Control. The wife takes over the checkbook and takes control of all financial matters. He turns over his paycheck to her every week. She attempts to plan more time for them to be together. Even though they are low on money, the wife buys tennis equipment in hopes of their taking up the sport to lessen the stress. The children are put on a tight budget and told to reduce the pressure on the father by being "real good." With all of the control attempts, the gambling still occurs. In desperation, the wife demands that either the gambling stops or she leaves.

Stage Four: Chaos. The gambling does not stop, but the wife fails to follow through in the threat of leaving. Even the children receive calls from loan sharks. Everyone's life is threatened. The family fears each day. They accuse the father of being a total failure. He considers suicide. The mother cannot function on her new job. The family is lost and without direction. No one knows where to turn. The school contacts the mother about the poor performance of the children.

Stage Five: Cancellation. The wife leaves and takes the children with her to a less expensive residence. She puts her best into her job to ensure adequate income for the family. The children stabilize under the mother's authority. But life is disrupted periodically when the gambling father begs to move in. The mother works twelve hours a day, trying for a promotion and more money. The children remain emotionally starved.

Stage Six: Compensation. Although repulsed by the thought of gambling, the wife enters her own game of chance. She has an affair with a married man. She gambles on not getting caught, and she plans to win. Unaware of her motives, she continues to feel empty and lost. The children also feel a great sense of loss. They become attached to a strong peer group. Their friends become their family.

Stage Seven: Creation and Recovery. The gambler begins attending Gamblers' Anonymous. The family attends with him from time to time. They also go to Alanon meetings. Everyone attends a recovery group of some sort. The father moves home and gradually takes charge of the finances again. As the family's trust in him increases, his self-confidence grows. The children feel the security of a family that is growing and maturing. They act out of choice, no longer driven by the problem.

6. Stealing. Problem: A daughter begins a habit of stealing and cannot stop without help

Stage One: Confusion. The mother is puzzled by the appearance of some new items of clothing in the girl's closet. The girl explains that she has been secretly saving the money for a long time. The mother remains puzzled and suspicious.

Stage Two: Cover-Up. Stores begin to call the mother requesting that she keep the girl out of their establishments or else they will file charges. The mother pays off the stores. The parents punish her and plead with her to stop. As rumors spread, the parents deny that the problem is any more than some of the girls involved in a prank. When asked about the stealing, both parents blatantly deny that anything is wrong.

Stage Three: Control. For the first time, the young girl is put in jail for shoplifting. The parents have long discussions on how to control the problem. Out of embarrassment the father seeks a job in another community, and the family moves. The girl promises that the stealing will never happen again. The family feels as if it is starting over.

Stage Four: Chaos. The girl steals a car and has a wreck in it. She is charged with a felony. The family is shocked and unable to take constructive action. The family members stop talking to one another to avoid the arguing and yelling that have increased since the theft.

Stage Five: Cancellation. The family essentially disowns the daughter. They agree with the juvenile justice system for her to be placed in a two-year minimum security youth camp for girls. The parents do not visit her. Their constant thought is of what she has done to them.

Stage Six: Compensation. The family feels a great sense of loss. One daughter sets out to make up for that loss. She tries for perfection but instead becomes a rigid young lady with unrealistic standards. All of the family problems are blamed on the problemed child. The father spends almost every evening with the guys at the bowling alley. He strives to increase his score, but his increase in alcohol consumption prevents that fron happening. The mother's career flourishes, as does her depression. The family feels little hope for ever being normal.

Stage Seven: Creation and Recovery. The family begins to make regular visits to see the daughter. The entire family enters therapy. Each member gradually is able to trust God to produce something good out of the tragedy. The parents become involved with other parents who have incarcerated children. They are patient for the family's healing process to take place. When the daughter is released, they all continue counseling together.

Codependency Is a Family Problem

The codependent family is a complex organization that starts with one person in trouble and progresses to the point that everyone is in trouble. In the progression, family members get locked into roles. Eventually the fulfillment of the role becomes more important than the development of family relationships. This progression happens in a predictable pattern of stages. Whatever the original source of the problem, there are similarities and parallels between them in every stage.

As the problem progresses from stage to stage, the stuck family is robbed of its choices. Even though the family's attempts to get unstuck have proven futile, the goal of the family usually has been to help the situation. But the harder the family struggles alone, the deeper into the progression it goes. Eventually the family members must be willing to do whatever it takes to stop the progression so that once again they will have freedom to decide.

One of the biggest roadblocks to the recovery of the family is that the members spend too much time and energy trying to control, hide, or find the cure to the problem. All their effort centers around the person who had the original problem. They think about the other person, not about their own personal problems that are developing. One person may initiate the recovery process, but treatment should involve everyone because recovery requires the whole family. The focus must be on the relationships, not on one person with one problem.

Another problem exists when the person with the identified problem is no longer with the family. Separation, divorce, or death may have moved the individual out of the family. Often families at this point see no need for treatment. They are blind to the development of other problems in reaction to the original one. But they are in great need of treatment. The unresolved emotions over the loss and destruction in the family send each member off on a course of compensation and survival rather than development and growth. If there is no way for the problemed member to return to the family, the family still needs help in the recovery process. Treatment can help each person introduce new knowledge into a new vibrant family.

Archaeological Digs Are Too Expensive

When families start treatment, they soon learn that the *cause* of their problem is much less important than its *resolution*. They have spent years trying to figure out why the problem occurred rather than learning what to do to resolve it. Treatment changes the family's priority from searching for reasons why to developing a plan for total recovery. The plan is generally a means of relapse prevention. This is essential since there is a tendency for family members to relapse into their old survival roles before the member with the original problem relapses into destructive behavior. As the family is able to center in on the present and let go of the past, the recovery process produces the desired goal of an unstuck family free from relapse.

It is rare that everyone in a family decides all at once to seek help. If it does happen, it is usually after a major crisis has brought the family together and to its knees. More frequently everyone struggles alone, wanting to do something and not knowing what to do. And in that struggle there is the false hope that if only one problemed family member could be "cured," then everything would be all right. Families do not have to wait for a cure that never happens. One person can initiate the recovery process.

Wanted: Professional Surgery

When one person decides to take action before others are willing, it is vital that a professional is sought who knows how to perform surgery on the problem. Chances are the member seeking help will need to intervene with other family members until they are all ready to intervene with the person with the original problem. These interventions are successful because of the power that is present in even the unhealthiest family relationships. But interventions are a delicate process. The more a person knows about a problem, the easier interventions become. One person in the family who is courageous enough to take action can move the family from stuck to starting over through the utilization of intervention specialists and techniques. But when that person moves into action, he or she must be certain that the professional sought out is experienced in intervening or can make a referral to a trained interventionist.

Even with professional help, drastic changes don't occur immediately. There are no easy answers for stuck families that have been struggling for years. No magical cure is available, nor are there perfect solutions. For some families, it takes years for evidence of recovery to be seen. For others, it is only months or weeks until a dramatic change is evident. Each family differs according to the intensity of the problem and the complexity of the damaged relationships. But for even the most problemed families, there is hope. That hope becomes available when someone in the family makes a decision to enter the recovery process.

The only alternative to recovery is for the family to stay stuck in a predictable progression toward the family's destruction. That progression is marked by disaster after disaster and ends in hopelessness. The cycle of destruction can be stopped with the willingness to change by one person. One courageous person can step out and lead the family toward recovery. In recovery is found the one thing missing from the stuck family. Hope.

From Disaster
to Disaster

A small town was inundated by flood waters. It was the biggest flood and the most exciting event that had happened in the town's history. A local newspaper reporter decided that he would set out on the waters to write a story. He located a small boat, climbed in, and proceeded to paddle out onto the river of water that had been a street just the day before. As he paddled his boat against the current, he noticed a woman sitting on the roof of a house. He paddled his boat to the edge of the roof, tied it up, and climbed out onto the roof. He introduced himself and, with her permission, pulled out his pad and pencil so he could record the events of the flood.

The first thing he noticed while watching the rushing waters flow by was a chicken coop full of fine poultry. So on his little pad he wrote, "Chicken coop full of fine poultry floated by." He continued his watch in hopes of a more newsworthy event. Not long afterward he saw a horse, broken loose from its tether, floating and swimming down the river. So he wrote in his little pad, "Horse, broken loose from its tether, floated by."

As he continued to watch for more articles or animals floating in the flood, he noticed, just in front of the house, a hat floating in the water. As he watched the hat float downstream with the current, he was startled. The hat floated just to the side of the house and made a distinct U-turn and floated upstream against the current. It was the most amazing thing he had ever seen. He watched more intently as he saw the hat float against the current to the opposite side of the house and make another distinct U-turn and again float back down the river with the current. Once again, he saw the hat make another U-turn at the side of the house and float back up against the current.

Bewildered, he asked the woman, "Do you have any idea what that hat is doing out there in front of your house?"

She replied, "I sure do. That's my husband. He said he was going to mow that lawn, come hell or high water."

Majoring on the Minors

The story illustrates an important point about us human beings. We often spend the majority of our time on the minor issues before us. We mow the lawn when the house is about to wash away. *We tend to ignore what is most important and focus on the trivial.* It is this trait of human nature that allows us to get stuck and stay stuck for a long time. If that were not serious enough, we also are frequently involved in enabling someone else to stay stuck too. We allow the person to deal with minor problems while major problems continue to worsen. The enabling causes stuckees and stuckors to get stuck deeper and stay stuck longer.

Yet most of us who are stuck to one degree or another can have hope. We are fortunate to be plagued with a malady from which there is a way out. But hope is available only if we are courageous. *We must develop the courage to cut from our lives whatever is preventing us from living the life we deserve.* We must cut what prevents us from living life to the fullest.

Without the courage to cut there is little or no hope. People who are afraid to change are the cowards of life. They are unwilling to look at themselves and say, "Hey, I am stuck and I need help!" For these people who lack the courage to change, there is little hope.

Often they are unaware of their hopeless condition because they are too busy trying to untie and untangle rather than cut. Their delay prevents recovery from starting. An alcoholic trying to drink socially is attempting to untie what must be cut. The overeater starting another fad diet is trying to untie a problem that must be cut. People die trying to untie what must be

111

cut. And as they die, they affect the lives of everyone around them.

Let's stop here to ask a basic question. What keeps everyone stuck? What entraps a person to a point where all control is lost? It is not one thing, but many things. People are stuck in *obsessions* that haunt them every day. They are burdened with *compulsions* that drive them to perform behaviors that are at times detestable. Some are stuck from *dependencies* and *codependencies*. They are dependent on people or things or possessions. And some are stuck because of a genuine *physiological addiction* to some type of chemical or substance like alcohol or drugs. The sources of being stuck are many and they grab us all at some point.

Because of so many causes of stuck, this section is devoted to explaining how human beings get stuck, stay stuck, and lose control. Losing control of life is a gradual process. It is a needless repetition of one problem after another, moving out of one disaster and into another. It is struggling to survive rather than living to grow.

Three Processes of Life

Life is at its best when we are actively involved in the three processes of life—becoming, relating, and achieving. These three processes occurring simultaneously and in balance offer the key to a fulfilling existence.

When becoming, relating, and achieving occur in balance, people around us are challenged to grow. One person's growth becomes the motivation for others. As this balance continues, it produces a synergism—a powerful sum of energy—where people are working, loving, and growing together. But in the course of life, these processes are interrupted by the unexpected, the unplanned. No one wants it to happen; no one really thinks it will. But it does. This something is *disaster*.

Disaster is the first entry into the cycle of destruction. Disaster comes in many forms. Some disasters are dramatic. Some are more subtle. An obviously dramatic disaster would be the loss of a child who died from illness or of a friend who died in a traffic accident. Marriage to an alcoholic is a dramatic disaster. And, of course, marriage itself can be a tremendous disaster. A

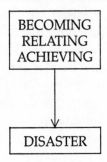

divorce can be even more traumatic than a disastrous marriage. Less dramatic, but no less traumatic disasters would include: loss of expectations, stress and pressures from job or family, change in roles or demands, an overwhelming sense of inadequacy in a fast-paced world, loneliness, or a feeling the world is not working out exactly as planned. These less dramatic disasters seem to gradually creep up on people.

Whether dramatic or not, these disasters do something to everyone who experiences them. Whatever the disaster, it results in an internal feeling that people do not like. In fact, some spend a lifetime avoiding it. The dreadful product of disaster is called pain. Personal disaster produces pain.

Most of us do not deal well with pain. Rather than process the pain, deal with it now, we tend to postpone or delay the pain. The attraction to immediate gratification drives people away from pain. It is human nature to separate an Oreo creme filled cookie and eat the smooth white inside first and the hard chocolate outside later. In a similar vein, human beings are bent on feeling good *now*. And if something unpleasant must be felt, people want to feel or experience the discomfort later. The most common reaction to emotional pain from disasters of life is to *postpone the pain.*

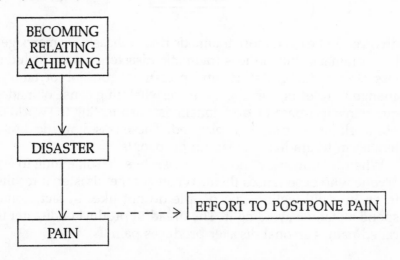

People are creative and diverse in their methods of postponing pain. Some people turn to the refrigerator to gorge themselves at the first hint of pain and discomfort. Others flee to the gambling tables or to the bookie in hopes of feeling the euphoria of a win. Lying, cheating, spending, or engaging repeatedly in unhealthy relationships are other methods of avoiding pain. Others become addicted sexually, where voyeurism, exhibitionism, or some other perversions become a practice. Still others use work, drugs, people, possessions, even religious fanaticism to dull the immediate feelings of pain.

Religiosity—Pill for Pain

In Texas, at a small psychiatric hospital, a preacher's wife in terrible shape became a patient. She was the mother of a very problemed child. She and her husband had shed many tears

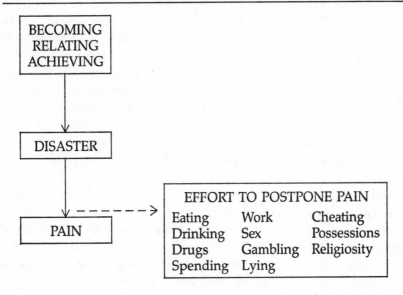

over their son who had become addicted to heroin. One night her son overdosed and died on the way to an emergency room. It was painful enough to admit that her son was a drug addict, given the profession of her husband. But dealing with the pain of losing her son to a drug overdose was more than she could handle, or more than she was willing to deal with at that particular time.

Shortly after the death of her son she began to exhibit unusual behavior. She would be found alone in a room, chanting one syllable over and over. She would be in a room full of people, and disregarding conversation in process, she would repeat prayers out loud. Her prayers made no sense. She was living in an unreal world of religious fanaticism that became more intense and less controllable.

Before being strapped to a stretcher and hurried to a mental facility, she had piled up all of the living room furniture in front of the fireplace. It was her intent to make an altar and offer a burnt offering to God in remembrance of her son. This poor woman was stuck. It was fortunate that she was taken to a place where she could receive help.

There are many others stuck in religious fanaticism to a lesser degree than the woman in Texas. They will never end up in an

115

institution. They will go through life repeating religious acts, not in an earnest attempt to know God, but in an attempt to avoid dealing with pain. It is common to hear these people state "I have a real peace about it" just after some tragedy has happened. In reality they are saying, "I'm simply not going to deal with the pain now." Fanaticism happens in many ways.

How Does Mr. Morality Wind Up in Jail?

Baylor University is a conservative Southern Baptist college in Waco, Texas. It is like any other school having a mixture of both "good" and "bad" students. What might be unique about Baylor is just how "good" the good students looked. One night, very late, I received a phone call from one of the good guys on campus. This guy could be called the best man on campus rather than the big man on campus. His reputation was flawless. People knew of him as extremely dedicated to living in accordance with some deep convictions. This image of Mr. Morality was known to many. He was a model student.

He called in the middle of the night and told me that he was in jail. I was shocked at the probable injustice that had been done to our model student. He asked me to bring down $150 cash for bail. It was beyond my imagination and my pocketbook. I was working at David Shellenberger's Men's Wear, and so I called David, explained the dilemma, and met him at the store where he loaned me the $150 for bail.

I drove to the police station, feeling guilty and nervous as if I had done something terribly wrong. I gave an officer the $150, and they released my friend. He sat down in the car, slumped in shame. Then he looked up at me and said, "I've got a problem." Well, that was an accurate evaluation of himself and the situation. Now I attempt to be an honest person, and I said, "You sure do!" He did have a problem, and he related it to me.

Ever since he was sixteen he had been fascinated by pornography. His uncle had introduced him to a library of hundreds of pornographic magazines. Soon his fascination turned into a full-blown obsession. Whenever he could sneak a look or spend hours studying the pictures, he found himself unable to control the urge. He was literally addicted to the feelings surrounding the acquisition and study of nude pictures.

He knew he had a problem, but he had kept it to himself since he was sixteen. He had done everything in his power to control himself. He would not even go into neighborhood grocery stores for fear of being trapped by an unavoidable magazine rack. He thought that marriage would help his problem become more manageable. And for a while it did. But soon after, he found himself searching out more secretive locations where he could safely purchase the pictures he desired. Every time he went after the pictures, he felt as if he was betraying his wife. His guilt was strong and he felt it deeply.

That night reality crept up on my friend and shattered his image of near perfection. He was in a large grocery store when the urge to look at the magazines hit him. He fought it for several minutes, but he finally found himself walking toward the magazine rack. He rationalized that just one walk in front of the rack would not hurt. Perhaps there would be a *Cosmopolitan* or some other "safe" magazine he could study.

The one harmless walk past the magazine rack turned into a nightmare. His close proximity to the pornography fanned the flames of his obsession. He could not resist the urge to pick up the magazines. So there he was, close to the campus where his image was beyond reproach. He could not get caught looking at them, and he could never walk up to the cashier and hand over the material and buy it. Someone might see him. As his passion raged, he desperately stuffed the magazines down his shirt and headed for the door. As he reached the door, a checker spotted him and summoned the manager, who grabbed my friend. There, in front of about fifty people, he had to pull the magazines out from under his shirt.

My friend was stuck, stuck in an obsession that had caused him agony for years. But on that night, the obsession drove him to commit an act against his own beliefs and values. The last thing he wanted to do was steal. It took this kind of experience, this hitting bottom, before the reality of his problem set in. He had to be arrested for shoplifting pornography before he could accept the need for help.

He did get help. His lovely wife had been aware of the prob-

117

lem but was convinced it was a thing of the past. She had moved from hurting inside to acceptance and then denial. Now she felt inadequate and guilty. And her husband had never felt guiltier.

Guilt had become a major complication in the development of the problem. Looking at the pornography had produced a lot of guilt inside the man. Pornography and guilt had become synonymous. So he turned to the pictures when he felt guilty, seeking some momentary, euphoric relief, only to be left with more guilt in the end. Because of the close association between the pictures and guilt, guilt fed the problem, and the problem fed the guilt.

My friend was caught in a common trap. Rather than deal with the pain of admitting that a problem exists, people postpone the pain. Unknowingly, they produce an even greater problem with greater pain and guilt. If my friend had been able to accept that he had a troublesome obsession, and had been willing to experience the pain of resolving the problem, he would have saved himself and his wife more misery.

Destructive behavior used to postpone pain produces guilt, anger, and fear. People feel as if progress is being made because the pain is less temporarily, but in fact, progress is being stalemated. They become engulfed by the unresolved emotions of guilt, fear, and anger.

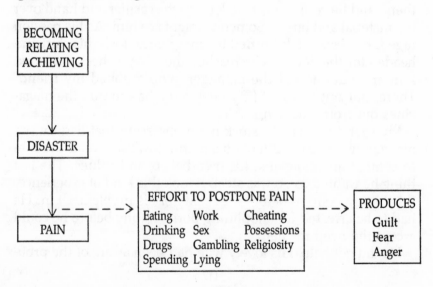

Guilt, anger, and fear can become deadly emotions. They must be dealt with head-on. When they are not resolved, they propel a person further into the cycle of destruction. They rob the individual of the ability to think and feel normally.

When we are stuck in some area such as eating, drinking, gambling, lying, or cheating, down inside us is a feeling of discomfort. We know that what is happening is going against some established value. Because the value system is violated, we feel guilt. The deeper into the behavior, such as overeating, the deeper the guilt. Guilt causes us to eat more, and the more we eat, the greater the guilt. *The trap is set by the behavior and secured by the emotion.*

As the problem grows, people close by tell us, "You should be able to control this," or "You're strong, you can handle these simple problems." Anger is internalized because we want to handle and control the problem, but we can't do it alone. So the anger grows as the frustration increases. Angry people become hypercritical of others. The whole personality becomes negative and insensitive to others. Anger is spread out into and onto others around us. As it spews out, less control is maintained. Both guilt and anger are reinforced as we have greater difficulty trying to stop or control the problem. The lack of direction offered by family and friends doesn't help.

We soon realize that a solution is not in hand. It also becomes evident that family, friends, and even many professionals do not have the answers. We begin to feel deserted by God or wonder if God even exists. All of this compounds the anxiety, progressing to the point where we fear ending up in a back ward of a mental hospital, insane or dead. Eventually, we become trapped in a pessimistic existence void of trust.

How Are Barriers Built Between Us?

Guilt, anger, and fear are the results of destructive behavior used to postpone pain. They are emotions to be reckoned with. They eat at us and destroy both mental and physical health. If not resolved they keep us moving in the cycle of destruction, producing a gap between what is and what ought to be.

Guilt, anger and fear, when left unresolved, also separate us from significant persons in our lives. These feelings have a tremendous capacity to divide the closest of relationships. When we feel guilt, anger, or fear, our tendency is to cover up and hide our emotions rather than share them. Anger is submerged beneath the surface for a long time before it is expressed in rage. Fear is a constant companion to many of us who have never had an anxiety attack or experienced terror. Guilt is not a feeling that is easily discussed openly. Instead, most of us create a protective shell or a barrier to hide behind. We succumb to the temptation to conceal, rather than force ourselves to reveal the feelings. Revealing the negative emotions initially is more painful, but it prevents relationships from deteriorating.

Deteriorating relationships get worse because barriers hiding the guilt, anger, and fear prevent honest, open communication between friends and family. Authenticity is lost when honest communication stops. A relationship simply cannot grow when one person is hiding or covering up feelings that need to be expressed. The more that is hidden, the wider the barrier between two people. As the wall thickens, the potential for growth lessens in the relationship, and two people move into mere coexistence rather than maturing companionship. Individuals are caught in acts of covering up and deception to promote the illusion that everything is wonderful. Left in the wake

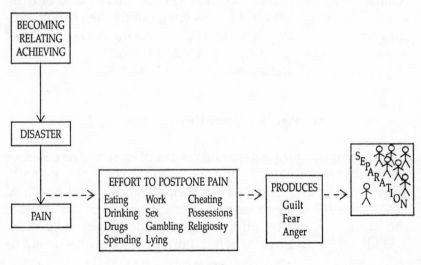

of this deception are broken relationships that died from lack of honesty.

The barriers that separate people and hide negative emotions come in many forms. Chemicals can be used as a means of total separation from reality and relationships. Overeating can produce an overweight condition that is an emotional and physical barrier combined into one. Certain professions can promote isolation. A psychologist, for instance, may appear close to people but may in actuality be repeating a situation throughout life where someone else is always the client or patient and he or she is always the professional. In the end, *destructive behavior produces emotions that cause separation.*

The Saga of Sophisticated Prostitution

A woman who presented herself as an expensive model was in reality a prostitute. But not the usual, street corner variety. This woman was a call girl who specialized in well-to-do business travelers. Her clients paid her $1,500 a night to go on trips and attend conventions with them. She was stuck, and her life was out of control. She exemplified how problems complicate and facilitate other problems.

In the truest sense, she was obsessed. She had come from a very poor family but had managed to attract a following of quite wealthy friends and boyfriends. As her exposure to their possessions continued, she became obsessed with material goods and money. She found herself willing to do anything to obtain more money and more possessions. "Anything" eventually encompassed sex.

When she started prostituting herself, she experienced tremendous fear, anxiety, and guilt. She hated what she was doing, but she loved the things that money bought and the power that came with it. Eventually, the fear and anxiety eroded and she began to look forward to her business encounters. Soon she found that she could not live without the repeated sexual experiences. She was trapped in a progressing sexual addiction. One problem had fed the other. Her ability to spend vast sums of money on automobiles, jewelry, and gifts was maintained by her lucrative sexual addiction.

The one thing that was not neat and tidy about her obsession with money and her addiction to sex was her tremendous guilt. Sometime in her childhood her parents had instilled in her some traditional values regarding sex, relationships, and responsibility. She had spent much of her life living in opposition to those values and daily violating her conscience. The guilt she felt was strong.

She also had what she called a "slight" drug problem. Her guilt was a painful emotion that she found could be eased with a chemical. Her physician had prescribed Valium for her agitation and inability to rest. She discovered that taken throughout the day, the Valium made the guilty pain more bearable. But what began as four ten-milligram Valiums a day grew to a thirty ten-milligram-per-day habit and addiction. Three hundred milligrams of Valium a day would keep most people in bed, but for her it was just enough to maintain. Her body had adapted to a heavy saturation of the chemical, and she knew that she could not function without it. It took six separate physicians and seven pharmacies to support her habit. She needed a way to get off the pills and stay off.

What was glaringly obvious about this woman was that she was void of any meaningful relationships. She was addicted sexually and had no one closer than those men she met as part of a business transaction. The walls and barriers that separated her from others were filled with pills, sex, money, gifts, and possessions. Surrounded by an image of wealth and security, she was isolated. She sought help only because of the physical withdrawal she experienced when she tried to cut down on the Valium. She exemplified what it means to be stuck.

Who Looks Good and Feels Bad?

When we become emotionally separated from family and friends, when we become unplugged from the reality of relationships, we compensate for the loss of those people and the loss of that nurturing. *The stronger the separation, the greater the need to compensate and cover up.* Life becomes layer upon layer of denial, illusion, and deception. We are masters at compensation. Any sense of loss, feeling of inferiority, or pain of emptiness can be covered by compensation. Compensation may come in many forms, but it always focuses on the external. Compensation results in the outside appearance being a distinct contrast from the inside reality. When there is no one to connect up with the feelings and the emotions on the inside, we make a drastic effort to fix up the outside.

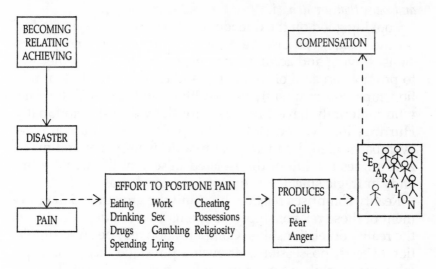

A common source of compensation is intellectualism—the process of talking about an issue rather than through a problem. Counselors, ministers, and others in helping professions constantly confront miserable people who intellectualize rather than deal with problems. For instance, if a physician becomes addicted to drugs and enters treatment, the doctor may spend hours talking about the addiction process and molecular composition of a chemical while avoiding the need to discuss his or her addiction and subsequent need for recovery. A fat person may spend hours reading about fitness and losing weight and be able to discuss the pros and cons of various weight loss methods, while avoiding entering the weight loss process. In short, people who intellectualize "talk a good game" but do not produce results.

The image of being an intellectual is often a ploy to keep people away. So often when we try to get close to someone, we are met with a barrage of information that prevents a relationship from growing or anyone getting close. The intimidation factor is so strong that no one would dare approach the person at a deeper, more meaningful level. All of this is played out in an effort to prevent being found out. It is a way of convincing everyone that all is well when it is anything but well. *The intellectualism is but an illusion that compensates for the misery and pain that are denied.*

Looking good on the outside, while everything is messed up on the inside, can also be achieved with money and possessions. Buying and accumulating expensive toys is another way to promote an aura of well-being and cover up the lack of relationships. But frequently the wealthiest in the crowd, the ones who materially have the most, are the weakest emotionally. Hurting, lonely, and isolated people are often surrounded, even barricaded, by their great wealth. Newspaper and magazine stories are full of the isolated misery of the wealthy that ends in tragic suicide or unexplained accidental death.

Reality comprises relationships and the growth and development of those relationships. Compensation is a departure from the reality of relationships. Compensation may be an accumulation of facts, possessions, or even a physique that promotes a false image while we continue to function in isolation. This unreality not only separates us from close relationships but also prevents us from accepting the present reality.

Shrinking Your Rearview Mirror

When we are unable to function in relationships and unable to handle the reality of the present, it is a logical step to turn to the past in search of comfort. The future becomes a source of fear and anxiety, the present almost ceases to exist. When we start to function in the past, we become rooted in the past, further eroding the ability to function in the present.

Driving an automobile is a good example of the need to deal appropriately with the reality of the present. Driving down the road at fifty-five miles per hour necessitates looking forward and being focused ahead. Reality is what we see approaching

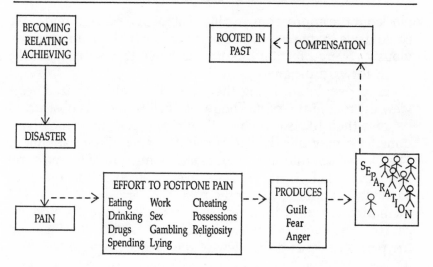

us. How well we deal with the reality just ahead at fifty-five miles per hour has everything to do with our ability to see tomorrow. We must be able to deal with the reality we see through the windshield in order to survive. We must face forward, ready to respond to whatever might be ahead.

Drivers need to maintain perspective and know what is approaching from the rear. To meet that need, a small rearview mirror is attached to the windshield of the car. It is small in comparison to the windshield because it is of much less importance, yet without it we could easily be run over by a semi before knowing anything was following too closely. It helps us stay ahead of disaster. The rearview mirror is essential for safe driving.

But imagine a car with a rearview mirror almost as large as the windshield:

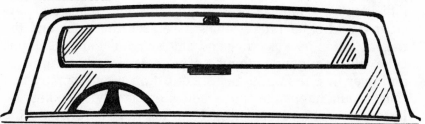

Drivers with oversized rearview mirrors would have little chance of a safe trip. The view of the rear would completely block out the approaching reality that must be encountered. We could drive in reverse and do fairly well at backing up over previously covered territory, but it's unlikely that we could make much forward progress.

Many people are living their lives through oversized rearview mirrors of the past. The reality before them is obstructed because their focus on where they have been, what they have done, and how they looked consumes most of their attention. They look back into their own rearview mirrors of the past, reliving every failure and studying every negative situation. With so much attention given to the past, they are able to learn and memorize the past, then repeat it, tragedies and disasters included. The cycle of destruction continues until the focus on the past shrinks and the view of the present expands.

Instead of Relate, Isolate

When we continue in a predictable cycle, repeating disaster after disaster, our isolation also continues to grow. This isolation results in distorted thinking, lack of assistance in resolving the problem, and ultimately the repeat of another disaster. As repeated disaster is seen in the individual, other disasters begin to crop up in the lives of family members. Consequently, an entire family becomes caught in the terribly destructive cycle. Everyone continues through life, never making progress, getting stuck in disaster after disaster, and continuously repeating the cycle of destruction.

This cycle is being played out in the lives of thousands of individuals and families every day. Counselors, ministers, physicians, and other professionals have seen this cycle and the tragedy left in its wake time and time again. For anyone in this cycle, life is sour and without meaning. As tragedy occurs over and over in one family, people question how so many bad things could happen to one person or one family. In taking case histories, young psychologists learn not to be surprised at the level of devastation revealed by an individual or a family. The stuck person and the stuck family are obvious by their pain and

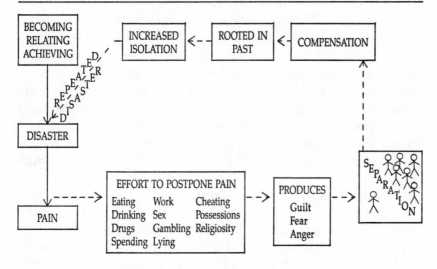

the ability to stack problem on top of problem. Recognition is not the problem, taking appropriate action is.

When a Family Is Not a Family, It's a Disaster

A man who weighed at least three hundred pounds appeared to have multiple problems, but his wife of sixteen years was his main concern. A very successful representative of an action sportswear line, she frequently traveled back and forth from San Francisco and New York, showing her clothing line and attending markets and shows. She had done very well in six years and was making over $100,000 a year. She also was addicted to cocaine which she had been using for five years.

This man had sought help because his wife's behavior was becoming unmanageable. Whenever she returned from a sales trip, she would plunge into a deep depression, not wanting to eat or talk to anyone. The least amount of irritation sent her into a fit of rage or a crying spree. The most disturbing behavior of all was that on some weekends she would not come home at all. This was unbearable for the husband and their two children. Her explanation was that she needed privacy because of the stress of her job. She promised that she would seek help if her ability to cope did not improve. After her repeated attempts to improve, and her continual failures, he called a counselor.

The husband knew it was a cocaine problem because of the evidence he found. Long before it was a problem she told her husband that she had tried it. That was five years earlier, and since then she had brought some home, even snorted some, while he watched. At first he was fascinated by the whole thing. But it gradually fed into his own insecurities which had erupted at the beginning of her successful career. They fought over the expense and over the days she was away from home until finally they stopped talking about it. His suspicions were verified when he found small bags of white powder in her purse. She constantly sniffed and unconsciously touched her nose; she spent thousands of dollars with nothing to show for it. With every new discovery of evidence came another promise from her to change. The change only went from bad to worse.

The man's weight problem had paralleled his wife's success and subsequent cocaine problem. Her success had augmented his insecurity, and he ate to cope. He had always had difficulty controlling his eating, but in the past two years he lost all control. He believed that once his wife had taken care of her problem, his weight would return to normal. He saw it as an outgrowth of the wife's addiction.

As for the impact on the children of an overweight father and an addicted mother, he denied that there was any problem. To him, his sixteen-year-old daughter and his fourteen-year-old son were unaffected. Both had gone through some moody periods and some very angry stages, but he claimed that things were back to normal. His sister who lived down the street from him had taken a lot of responsibility for the kids as his wife's career and drug problem kept her away from home. The children loved their aunt and stayed with her frequently.

He wanted to find a simple plan that would dramatically change his wife's behavior and bring some normalcy back to the family. The plan suggested to him was neither simple nor was it what he expected or wanted to hear. If there was to be any hope for the family or his wife, he needed to do three things that were difficult but essential.

The first action was for him to check into an eating disorders unit. Since his sister could take care of the kids, this was possible. His problem was severe, and the sooner he started working on it, the better. He was in no condition to motivate his wife toward change until she saw him make a serious move to help himself. If he went to an eating disorders unit, his family would be involved in the treatment. This would be an excellent means of facilitating recovery for the entire family.

Second, he needed to attend Overeaters Anonymous. Although treatment would introduce him to Overeaters Anonymous, he needed to know from the beginning that it was a vital part of a successful recovery program.

Third, he needed a family therapist who could work well with the children and attempt to pull the family back together.

He was encouraged to get his wife to talk to a counselor, but his disappointment was obvious. He had expected answers to change his wife, not himself. He had thought that her changing would provide the motivation for him to change. He did not expect that it would have to be the other way around. He was unwilling even to discuss what had been proposed.

Four months later he again sought counseling, but this time his wife was with him. She was unwilling to discuss either her problem or her husband's problem. She was there to discuss their sixteen-year-old daughter. The previous week she found the girl in her bedroom with a boy that neither of the parents had met. The mother had been awakened at 3:00 A.M. by her daughter's giggling. The two young people were completely naked, lying on the bed drinking whiskey straight out of the bottle. She felt that somehow she had lost control over her daughter. She was unaware that her daughter had ever had a drink before, nor had she ever discussed sex. The shock of the scene was more painful than anything she had ever experienced. She said she would do anything to help her daughter.

It was suggested that in order for her to help her daughter she needed to do three things: (1) check herself into a drug treatment center, (2) attend Cocaine Anonymous or Narcotics Anonymous, and (3) get in touch with a family therapist to try to pull the family together. Again the father was told to check into an eating disorders unit, attend Overeaters Anonymous, and start seeing his own therapist. It was also recommended that their daughter receive counseling. They were unwilling to take action and were disinterested in this plan.

Disaster after disaster after disaster was being repeated throughout the family. If any family was stuck in a cycle of destruction, it was this one. They desperately needed to stop attempting to control the problems and to move into action to solve them. They felt the problem that needed solving first was the daughter. So rather than the entire family's getting involved in the recovery process, they fought the problems and one another. The sadness I felt when I learned of this family was deep. Their situation did not improve.

The final disaster was the worst tragedy of all. Their fourteen-year-old son walked into the living room, put a .22 caliber pistol to his temple, and pulled the trigger. The father came in, saw what had happened, put the gun to his head, and shot himself too. The father survived. There in a hospital room was a family stuck in the cycle of destruction. But not until after the death of the young boy were they willing to do whatever it took to recover.

Rarely does a family reach the depths of this one. Yet every family who is in the cycle of destruction is capable of experiencing tragedies similar to this family. This extreme case illustrates the natural consequences of doing nothing about problems. Even when people feel they are making progress due to some temporary change or temporary result, the predictable progression of repeated disasters continues.

It is vital for the family not to be fooled by temporary changes that offer nothing but false hope. Attempting to resolve the problem with a new scheme alone leads to yet greater disappointments and the continuance of the cycle. The key to identifying whether results are temporary rests in relationships with people. If the solution is sought alone, the results are short lived. If the solution is sought in supportive relationships with others, where problems are shared and feelings expressed, the results are solid hope for a strong recovery. Recovery is short lived in isolation.

The cycle of repeated disaster, tragedy, and trauma is full of broken relationships and isolated people in pain. The wasted time spent on maintaining control rather than resolving the problem is totally unnecessary. At any point a person or a family can decide to move out of the cycle of destruction and enter the process of recovery. The first step to stopping the cycle and ending the damage is to recognize the need to do so. To be able to admit that there is a problem that needs help is the point at which recovery can begin. When deadly denial ends, a new life can begin. For people who are stuck, the beginning can be now.

Starting Over

If for some reason a person told you that you were a horse, it would be best just to ignore it. If a second person were to call you a horse, it would be cause for concern. It would be worth looking into. But if three people were to call you a horse, then maybe it would be time to buy a saddle.

If the symptoms and indicators of being stuck start to mount up, then it is time to "saddle up" and start over. But what are the symptoms and indicators that point to being stuck in the cycle of destruction? What are the key points that represent the need to take immediate action? This chapter answers these questions and provides the first three steps in moving from stuck to starting over.

It's Time to Saddle Up

. . . When the Undesirable Increases

Problems are indicated by compulsive patterns that increase in frequency and produce undesirable consequences. Life should be a process of doing more and more of what produces desired results. It should not be a repetition of doing things that produce undesirable results. As people mature, behaviors that produce undesirable results should be eliminated and replaced with behaviors that result in the desirable.

Compulsive eating and drinking are examples. When a heavy person gets heavier because of compulsive eating, when that person continues to eat uncontrollably and gain more weight, and when that person hates more and more to look in the mirror with the addition of every new pound, that person is caught in a destructive cycle. Crash diets that reduce weight for two months are indicators of the same problem when the weight is replaced with even more fat in four months. The diet that produces temporary results is undesirable. It only prevents the desired state of normal weight from occurring.

Many alcoholics, when asked about the effects of drinking, will relate pleasurable feelings of warmth, security, and euphoria. They fail to mention the broken marriage, disturbed children, morning-after sickness, or the pleading, yelling, and screaming that often accompany a drinking binge. Even if it has been twenty years since the drinking has provided pleasurable memories, alcoholics will hold on to the belief that alcohol continues to produce desirable results.

As undesirable results and repeated tragedies mount up, people rationalize that life is tough and full of sorrow. Well, it may be, but so often the tragedies can be avoided with a change in behavior due to the recovery process. When undesirable results increase, rather than accepting that it is "just life," the person is better off asking, "What am I doing to contribute to this?" Accepting responsibility for correcting the problem comes from admitting that a specific behavior not only produces undesirable results but also increases the frequency of the undesirable.

. . . When You Feel a Need to Control

Problems are indicated by repeated attempts at control that end in relapse. When something is not a problem, we do not have to control it. Few people must control the urge to eat carrots. Why? It is not a problem. People who have a problem with gambling attempt to control the gambling. Men who have a problem with extramarital affairs attempt to control the urge to sleep with women other than their wives. Alcoholics attempt to control their drinking, and workaholics attempt to control their time away from home. Problem areas are obvious to objective observers. Areas that need control are problem areas, and they indicate that a person is stuck in the cycle.

. . . When You Are Filled with Anguish

Problems are indicated by repeated frustration and short-term results from attempts to control the behavior. Anguish lives where hope is dying. It is caused by a complete lack of direction in resolving the problems that increase in intensity. Because repeated attempts to control the problem produce only short-term results, anguish sets in. It flourishes in the midst of conflicting advice from family and friends.

Anguish is pain combined with anxiety. The person feeling anguish fears the future because in addition to intensification of the problem, the consequences of the problem causes pain. The harder the efforts at controlling the problem, the greater the anxiety and pain. Living in anguish is like having a dark cloud hovering above. It grows into the belief that to be alive is to be miserable.

Everyone has problems. But when normal problems are combined with anguish over more severe problems, the results can be devastating. In an effort to cope, people often drink heavily or seek relief through a drug of some sort. This compounds the problem and feeds the anguish already in existence. Problem upon problem piles up to make misery more miserable. A simple problem causes frustration, but repeated problems produce anguish beyond frustration and life without hope.

. . . When You Experience Withdrawal

Problems are indicated by the immediate urge to repeat compulsive behavior that is stopped. When a person in the cycle of destruction stops a compulsive behavior, that person has an immediate urge to repeat the behavior. This urge is called withdrawal. Withdrawal often dashes the hopes of stuck people who are attempting to resolve problems on their own. When will power is mustered up, the person makes the decision to change and finally stops the behavior. Withdrawal drives the person into starting again.

Smoking, drinking, abusing drugs, and eating have some

chemical withdrawal involved that makes the withdrawal problem more complicated. But with some problems, the emotional attachment is stronger than chemical addiction. Someone caught up in an extramarital affair knows the agony of withdrawal when attempting to stop the unhealthy relationship. Emotional withdrawal can be so intense that it makes the person physically ill, as if there were a chemical withdrawal also. Whether it is the need to stop having a relationship or to stop making trips to the refrigerator, withdrawal and the urge to repeat the negative act indicate that the cycle has its grip on the person.

. . . When There Are Repeated Disasters

Problems are indicated by repeated tragedies that result in still more tragedies or disasters. It is obvious that a person is in the cycle when tragedy results in still more tragedies or disasters. Repeated tragedies cannot be passed off as mere bad luck. When a family is riddled with personal problems—such as financial crises, teen-age drug abuse, divorce, and legal problems from tax evasion—it is no accident or quirk of fate. It is the result of a family stuck in a cycle of destruction. The cycle begins by entrapping first one family member and then trapping the entire family. When the entire family becomes a disaster, one or all are stuck in the cycle.

. . . When You Feel the Brick Walls of Isolation

Problems are indicated by walls that are thrown up to keep others out. The opposite of being *Hooked on Life* is going through life in isolation. Loneliness is not the normal condition for human beings. It is abnormal for people to increase their isolation through working too much or changing residences or always having to lead.

Alienation from others makes people feel as if everyone else is different, that no one understands or could understand. Alienated people fear relationships, and they fear pain that has resulted from destructive relationships in the past. Alienation and the state of isolation are the exact opposites of recovery.

135

Since recovery cannot happen in a vacuum, alienation can only bring about more tragedy and misery.

People who experience alienation are often surrounded by people. They appear to be active and involved. But a closer look reveals that there is no communication going on. There is sharing of information without any personal sharing of one another. Being surrounded by people is not a protector from alienation. Sometimes it feeds it.

For a lot of people, it is time to "saddle up" and get on the road to recovery. When the evidence piles up and points to a serious problem that intensifies day after day or year after year, it is time to do something about the problem. But moving out of the cycle or that comfortable rut takes courage. It takes courage to be willing to cut from your life that which is preventing the desirable from happening. It seems that it would be a simple choice to move out of a cycle of destruction and move into recovery. But it is a complicated system of unhealthy dependencies that locks a person in, that destroys the willingness to cut off the problem. *Seldom is the decision for recovery reached alone. It takes supportive people around the stuck person to assist in the transition from stuck to starting over.*

Three Steps to Starting Over

Human nature goes against our need to start over. For recovery to begin, we must force ourselves to go against the more natural things and move into what it takes to change. It is human nature to hide problems, to cover them up and not talk about them. It is natural to take the path of least resistance, to do what is easiest at the time. Getting unstuck is never easy. It goes against the natural reactions that have compounded the problem. It takes courage.

Step One: Confession—Courage to Open Up to Another

This first step is an old concept. People really don't like to talk about it. It has been reclassified through time and labeled old-fashioned and unnecessary. But it is vital to the healing process. Covering up and hiding problems make people sick. Uncovering problems and becoming open make people well. As an individual gradually is able to reveal more and more about problems, layers of isolation and alienation can be shattered.

Self-revelation and confession is a gradual process, like peeling an onion layer by layer. It must be done carefully and cautiously. Too much too soon only leads to more problems. When years of troubles have been bottled up and concealed and then carelessly spewed out to a friend, it is embarrassing to both individuals. This only increases the alienation. When the walls of concealment are dropped quickly, they are usually stronger when reconstructed.

Confession is really nothing more than agreeing with someone that a problem exists. It is not revealing every indiscretion that has ever happened with all of the details. Denial causes disagreement when confronted by the consequences of a problem. When denial stops, confession can begin. When done properly, confession can be a tremendous relief as openness starts to develop between two people. As the sharing gradually increases, a new freedom is experienced by the one who has suffered alone for too long.

Problems with sex are perhaps the most frequently hidden problems of all, especially problems from the past that constantly creep up on a person and cause self-doubt and self-incrimination. The frequency with which people cover up and stay stuck in this area is of epidemic proportions. People frequently find that simple revelation can heal the past.

After I spoke one evening, a man came up to discuss a problem he had been struggling to handle. I had known him for a couple of years. He had a bright wife and a brand-new baby. He told me he was stuck with a problem that he could not resolve. It was a sexual problem, not of action but of thought. He reconfirmed his great love for his wife to me, then he shared the difficulty. Before he was married he had had sexual relationships with many women over a period of years. He said that he had never told anyone before but that he was constantly obsessed with thoughts and images of sexual relationships he had experienced before marriage. The more he tried to stop thinking about them, the greater the frustration he felt. The memories were deeply ingrained and he wanted help, but he did not know what to do or where to begin.

I discussed the problem with him a little further and reassured him that he had just begun to take care of the problem. His courage to open up about the problem at the risk of destroying his image would lead him to relief from the dreaded thoughts. I gave him the name of a person to contact. Shattering the isolation with open confession is the first step back to health and into recovery.

Another example is far more severe and sad. A woman named Helen had spent about twenty years in and out of mental institutions. When she was a young girl she was abused and frequently sexually molested by her father. In order to convince her not to tell her mother, the father frequently gave the little girl gifts that she loved. She never told her mother about the attacks from her father.

Her feelings of guilt had closed her off from her mother and began to separate her from all other relationships in her life. Her guilt grew, and as it did, her alienation increased. The first psychiatrist she saw at a mental health clinic admitted her to a state mental hospital. Her condition worsened to a level of paranoia and fear of others that made her suspect everyone of wanting to harm her. Her first admission to an institution provided her with something she had sought, separation from the real world. That separation had been further enhanced over the years with the use of major tranquilizers and other neuroleptic medications that affected the nervous system. In all of her attempted treatments, she had never revealed the incest with her father.

In a small psychiatric hospital in Texas, years after her first admission into a mental institution, a remarkable thing happened. A young assistant working there was able to establish instant rapport with patients. This chubby, bearded man was able to break through in some of the most difficult cases. He began working with this extremely troubled woman and discovered that she felt as if others were flawless in comparison to her. She focused on her inferiority rather than being able to express the real problem behind the inferiority. So the assistant gradually began to share some of the problems that he had experienced. He attempted to convince her that everyone has secrets that are concealed behind their facade of false security.

Eventually she was able to believe that she was not the only person with some terrible, ugly memory from the past. The more the assistant shared and confessed about himself, the more she was able to share and confess about herself. Finally she was able to talk about and reveal the incestuous relationship that she had with her father. She talked of her lifelong guilt from concealing the episodes from her mother. She even went on to admit her enjoyment of the gifts from her father. Finally she reached a stage of accepting responsibility for not resolving the past and continuing in a "crazy" world.

As these revelations unfolded, everyone in the facility began to notice the emergence of a new person. Her appearance changed from the expressions on her face to what she wore. Her newfound relief could be sensed by everyone. As time went on she was discharged from the hospital and went out to start a new life. It was a remarkable recovery that began with the confessions of an assistant that prompted the confessions from a deep, dark past. The covering and hiding had produced years of illness. The openness and confession had produced healing and wellness. It was the key to a new life of recovery.

Too many people are stuck today because of their unwillingness to open up and confess problems. Small, even insignificant problems can grow in severity because people hide and conceal them. Pride prevents people from admitting their own humanness and ability to stumble or to fail. Humility, instead of pride, allows a person to be free of the problems of the past through the process of admitting and confessing irresponsibilities. The biggest irresponsibility of all is the unwillingness to confess the little ones. Confession unlocks the freedom and the relief that are available to anyone who is stuck. But confession is just the first step.

Step Two: Communication—Courage to Relate Within a Group

Communication within a supportive community is the second step. It must be an ongoing process for recovery to be secure. It is more than just a one-time confession of irresponsi-

bility. It is also a discovery of the real person beneath the facade. Communication within a supportive community involves
facing reality and expressing emotions that evolve from that reality. It is the ability to listen and to accept others as they express different feelings about the same reality.

A supportive community can come in many different forms
and sizes. It might be called a self-help group, a growth group,
a recovery group, or a therapy group. Whatever the name, or
whether it has three or thirty people, the supportive community is made up of individuals who are willing to admit that
they are all strugglers together in this world and that the struggling is made easier when openness and honest communication form the base of relationships. And in these relationships
there is accountability to one another.

I was fortunate to be a part of a group where there was a
healthy balance between support, confrontation, and accountability. One of the members was a man recovering from compulsive gambling who stayed away from betting for about five
months. The group noticed, however, that his contributions to
the group had become superficial. Something was going on beneath the surface that he was not sharing. One of the women
finally confronted him by telling him that he was avoiding dealing with real issues. She was holding him accountable.

He resented her words, and he denied that he had any new
or extraordinary problem. We all felt empty when the session
ended. The following week, we started the group by talking
about how we had felt the week before. The group expressed
concern for the group member who was avoiding the reality of
his life. The man's head dropped, and he began to cry. He cried
for several minutes. Then he revealed his suspicions that his
wife was leaving him. She did, eventually, and he survived. He
survived because he had a place where he could be open and
supported. The openness had begun because someone cared
enough to confront him and hold him accountable to the group.

The supportive community provides a place where communication can be practiced and improved. It is a place where
people not only confess their irresponsibility but also learn to
communicate support and encouragement for others. It is a
place to discover that others have experienced many of the
same problems and have survived, and to hear their insight

from having overcome the difficulties. Communication with a supportive community is vital for recovery. To be able to open up and reveal problems, even when it is difficult and painful, is a survival skill that must be developed. Without this skill, this ability to communicate, recovery is only temporary.

Step Three: Commitment—Courage to Do Whatever It Takes

Commitment to do whatever it takes is the third step in starting over. It involves the courage to cut out of life whatever is preventing the achievements that are desired and deserved. Commitment means to stop trying to convince the world that the problem can be handled alone. Doing whatever it takes involves working with others toward recovery rather than attempting to solve the problem alone. Commitment to do whatever it takes is the ability to say, "I'm stuck, and I'm ready to do whatever it takes to get rid of the problem." Commitment is made of courage.

Commitment to the convenient will never do. Courageous commitment to do whatever it takes is a necessity for recovery. Often a lifetime is spent attempting to untie and untangle problems that need to be severed. Whatever is standing between hope and recovery must be cut off as soon as possible, no matter how painful.

The courage involved in commitment can be illustrated by a story[1] from a logging camp in the backwoods of Oregon. In order to transport logs from the top of the mountain down to the river below, the loggers constructed large wooden chutes. They would cut down a tree, strip off the limbs, then place the huge trunk in the chute and slide it down to the river. By the time the logs reached the river, they were traveling very fast. They would hit the water, then float down the river to the mill.

The loggers used the wooden chutes to save time and effort in getting from the top of the mountain to the bottom. Rather than walk to the bottom, they would place an ax in the chute and ride down on the handle. It saved time and it was exciting and fun.

One day a logger slid down the chute on his ax handle and

1. Robert A. Raines, *Creative Brooding* (New York: Macmillan, Inc., 1977).

attempted to get out of the chute when he reached the bottom. But when he stood up, he slipped. His foot became lodged in between two of the large wooden planks that made up the chute. It was wedged in tight. As he struggled frantically to pull it out, he heard the yell, indicating a huge tree trunk was being sent down, from on top of the mountain. In desperation he struggled harder, trying to get out of his boot or free the foot. But there he stood, his foot caught in the planks, the huge trunk speeding toward him, and all he had was his ax. He was stuck, and the only way out took courage from within. That man had the courage to cut from his life the only thing that stood between him and death. He axed off his foot and jumped free in time to save his life. Many would have died trying to untie a boot that would not come free.

Attempting to untie and untangle what must be cut has caused many deaths or other tragedies. It has kept people in the cycle of destruction and destroyed their ability to live freely. But there comes a time when a person must say, "I have eaten enough!" or "I have drunk enough!" or "I have bought enough!" When that point is reached, confession, communication, and commitment can move the person from the cycle of destruction into recovery.

Where the Nitty Gets Gritty

The most critical point in the cycle is found when a person attempts to postpone pain rather than process it.

An individual may have false hope that if the pain is put off or delayed, it will go away. But in reality, delayed pain becomes more painful. It is like one of the automobile repair ads that has a mechanic saying, "You can pay me now, or you can pay me later." Pain must be dealt with and resolved now, or it will produce further problems, become more painful, and keep a person stuck in the cycle of destruction. In fact it has been said that postponing pain is the source of all neuroses. But eventually a person reaches a point when he or she has been through enough disasters that compound the pain. Finally the person stops postponing the pain and starts processing it.

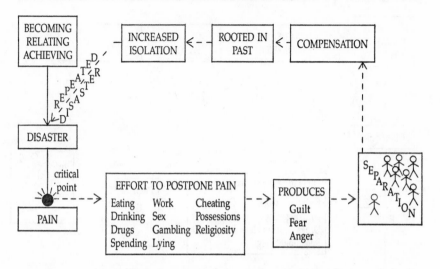

Confession, communication, and commitment provide the force and power to break out of the cycle of destruction and begin processing the pain. Everyone is going to experience tragedy or disasters that produce pain. Pain comes from loss. It may be loss of comfort, loss of a family member, or loss of expectations. What hurts so deeply is that life differs greatly from expectations. And when it does, people retreat into a repetition of "if onlys": "If only I had been better"; "If only I had never made that mistake." It is as if had things been different, life would have worked out as expected and been free of pain. Processing the pain involves accepting pain as an integral part of human existence.

Pain must be felt. Alcohol, sex, drugs, food, or work may deaden it temporarily, but it must be felt. It also must be expressed. Part of the ongoing communication involves expressing the feelings of pain that have been disguised or hidden. When this happens, a person is able to expand his or her world and become more than before the pain began. When a parent has a child that dies, the pain is probably greater than any other tragedy could produce. That parent must fight the temptation to eat through the pain or drink through the pain. The parent also must fight the tendency to suffer alone. The parent must make a concerted effort to feel the pain, express it, and grow from it. Then the parent can handle other problems more easily

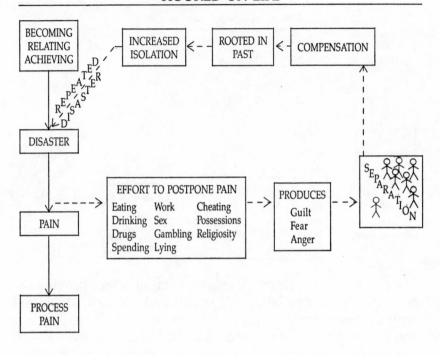

and assist other people in growing. Growth occurs because of the pain rather than in spite of it. Growth comes from resolution of the pain rather than giving in to the urge to delay processing the pain.

When resolution of pain is complete, the pain becomes a point of reference and not a predictor of the future. Within the person is a memory of the depth of the feeling, but the pain is no longer felt in all of its intensity. It is resolved to become a memory of the past rather than a present reality. Resolution of pain also involves the ability to forgive. Forgiveness of self, God, others, or life itself must occur for the pain to be totally resolved. Forgiveness must be offered up to others who have been the source of hurt, and it must be accepted and received openly from those who have been hurt. The pain will never be

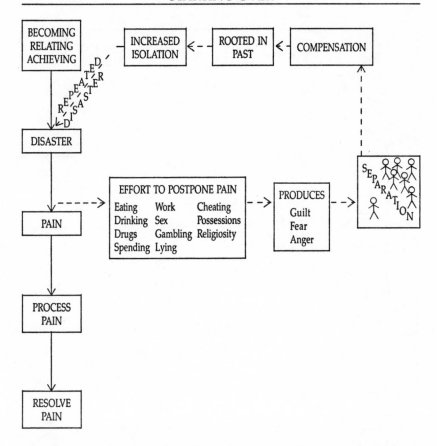

forgotten, but if not forgiven, it cannot be resolved. When pain resolution continues, the individual can then experience ongoing growth and recovery.

Growth and recovery is a return to a balanced development of the three processes—becoming, relating, and achieving. Once out of the cycle, a person can resume personal development, increasing the quality of relationships and pursuing achievements that fit into a well-defined purpose. Achievement for achievement's sake is replaced with accomplishments that are a part of a new life mission. That life mission has been expanded by the painful experiences that provided growth and maturity. As disaster, tragedy, and pain are processed and resolved, the person's world is expanded into new and exciting areas.

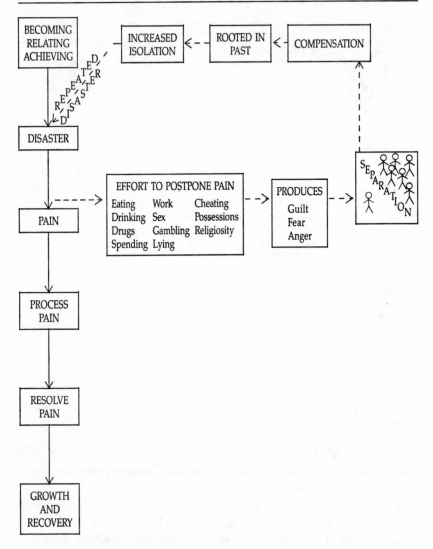

Newspapers and magazines abound with examples of individuals who have turned a tragedy or trauma into a new life mission. Recovering alcoholics have built treatment centers to help motivate others. Crime victims have started groups so that other victims may receive help and begin again. Young people who have lost limbs to cancer have hobbled across this country to raise money for research so that a cure can be found and others can receive help. These brave new crusaders have a common thread running through their experience. Disasters be-

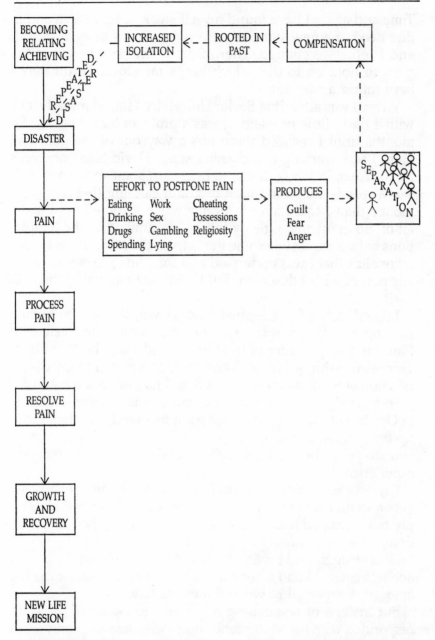

came their starting points for new life missions. As a result, rather than one wasted life, thousands of lives have been recovered.

For me, life has been a continual process of starting over.

Time and again I have found myself stuck in some area and in dire need of a new start. Like everyone else, I deny, I protest, and I refuse to change. Then, finally, the pain becomes too great to hold on to that which keeps me stuck. Fortunately I have found a way out.

When I was attending Baylor University I found myself stuck with a nasty little problem. It was a problem that ate at me for months until I realized there was a way out of the guilt and pain. I was working at a clothing store, David Shellenberger's Men's Wear, in Waco, Texas, to help earn some extra money. It was a wonderful store full of beautiful clothing that cost more money than I could afford. Money was not something I had a lot of. So gradually, little by little, I succumbed to the temptations before me. I stole some items from the store. I was able to rationalize that I was underpaid and that the clothes were actually part of what I deserved. But I could not rationalize the guilt I felt.

Immediately I felt alienated from David, the owner. I could no longer look him in the eye or communicate effectively with him. He had put a lot of trust in me and I had betrayed him. Our relationship grew more and more strained, and my dissatisfaction at working there intensified. I had no idea what to do.

Fortunately for me, my parents had enrolled me in a seminar in October of that year. I did not want to attend, but they drove up from Bryan to attend the sessions with me. I hung in there and attended the sessions until the end. It was a life-changing experience.

One of the seminar's key points that struck me between the eyes and hit every joint of my body concerned confession. Simply put, I needed to do it. If I were to experience personal freedom, I had to confess to my boss that I was a thief. So after a time of struggle and procrastination, I went to him and told him about the items I had taken and handed him a check for the full amount. I expected to be fired immediately.

But instead of responding in anger, the owner of the store responded with understanding and forgiveness. Not only was I not fired, but he viewed me with new respect. He allowed me to work closer with him than ever before.

It was not long after that time that I began to speak to civic groups and tell the story of confession and how it renewed our relationship. Careers were affected as others took the risk of opening up and confessing to some indiscretion. Others experienced freedom as the burden of guilt was lifted. Bosses and employees were able to renew their relationships. It was a new beginning for me.

I would like to be able to say that that was the worst thing I've ever done or that since that time my life has been spotless, but it just is not so. Fortunately, however, each time I have become stuck or trapped, I have been able to tap in to the freedom that is available simply by admitting that I have been wrong. In addition, I have been able to watch others do the same and develop their own new life mission out of the refuse and debris of imperfect living.

Opportunity abounds for people who are stuck and possess the courage to start over. Starting over can be the beginning of a new life more beautiful and more meaningful than ever imagined. One person's problems can be the source of inspiration for others who experience similar problems and work to overcome those problems. It all begins with admitting that a problem exists and confessing that problem openly and honestly to another person. Followed by honest communication and the commitment to do whatever it takes, these three steps begin the recovery process. In recovery, a person processes the pain, resolves it, and grows from it. This growth expands the person's world and allows a new life mission to form. This new life mission serves as a motivation for others to start over and move out of the cycle of destruction.

Stuck people stay stuck because they believe some magical solution is going to resolve life's problems. Recovery is available to everyone, but it is not chosen because of the false hope that things will get better. How much more suffering must someone experience? How many more disasters must leave a path of destruction? How much more pain and hopelessness must be felt before choosing the pain that produces growth and maturity? Only the stuck person can answer these questions. But when that point is reached when the suffering has gone on long enough, the process of recovery can begin. All that is needed is the willingness and courage to do whatever it takes.

Growing Yourself Up
All Over Again

A new lawyer set up shop in a new office building. He had a sign painted on his door announcing his new law practice. It was a great day that he had worked extremely hard to reach. He had a desk, a chair, a couple of client chairs, a small file cabinet, and a telephone sitting upon the desk. All that was missing was clients—paying clients.

As he sat back in his chair wondering how to market his new profession, he heard footsteps in the hall. The only thing he could think was, "My first client!" He quickly picked up the phone and acted as if someone were on the other end of the line, one of his many clients. He faked a conversation and said, "Yes, of course I can. I can help you do all of that. Oh, sure, I have worked on all kinds of cases from the least to the most complex." The person who was coming down the hall finally appeared in the doorway, leaned against the frame of the door, and waited for the new lawyer to acknowledge him.

"Oh, of course, I will be glad to help in any way I can," the lawyer continued. "Could you hold just a moment?" The lawyer put his hand over the mouthpiece of the phone and said to the man in the doorway, "Can I help you with anything?" "Yeah," the man said, "I'm from the telephone company. I've come to hook up your phone!"

Our attorney friend was faking it, just as many do with life. Instead of being hooked on life, people become stuck on the way to life. Faking life is no way to live.

In order to continue moving toward starting over (recovery) you must learn what it means to "grow yourself up all over again." The recovery process begins when you stop compensating for your problems and you re-enter the three processes of life—becoming, relating, and achieving.

Priorities: First Things First

There are no shortcuts in the growing up process. When it comes to life, a shortcut is the *longest* distance between two points. Before considering the processes of becoming, relating, and achieving in growing up, let's prioritize them.

Priorities don't necessarily refer to quantity of time, but rather to quality of time. Unless there is sufficient quantity of time, quality time will not emerge. Within the three universal processes of life there are priorities. The first priority is the process of becoming, to know who we are. This is the moral basis for life. The next priority is the process of relating. As we discover who we are, we learn to cultivate intimate relationships. Then what we think of ourselves (becoming) and how we relate to others (relating) form a most healthy foundation for the third priority, the process of achieving. This process encompasses our vocational/community responsibilities. Our long-term effectiveness here depends directly on the higher priorities of becoming and relating. Too often, the processes of life are reversed—achieving, relating, and then becoming—which dramatically stunts the growth process. This is where stuck people live.

Priorities offer guidelines or levels of long-term importance. From the long-term perspective, our intimate relationships (process of relating) are far more important than our vocational/community responsibilities (process of achieving), but understanding who we are (process of becoming) is even more important than our intimate relationships (process of relating). These three life processes, in priority order, form universal guidelines for full recovery.

Growth Step #1:
How to Re-Enter the Process of Becoming

All of us desperately need to experience the life processes because that is what makes us whole and healthy. Even though we get stuck and frustrate that desperate need, we can and must re-enter these processes.

First, re-enter the process of becoming! If you do that, you re-enter reality. Facing reality is awfully tough. Probably the toughest reality that you will ever face is that *you are the product of your choices*. If you are stuck, you have the power to get unstuck (to start over) simply by your own *choosing*.

No matter how you arrived at stuck, you must choose to start over. You may or may not have chosen loneliness, but you have the power to choose not to be lonely. You didn't choose for your loved one to die, but you, and only you, have the power to choose to go on with life. You may not have consciously chosen the disease that plagues you, but you have the power to choose to handle it. You may not have desired that divorce, but you do have the choice of recovery from the relational wounds. You may feel that you are a victim of anorexia or overweight, of alcohol or drugs, of gambling or smoking, of sick relationships or no relationships, but you have the power of life and living or death and dying within your power to choose.

Stuck people have two major problems in making choices! First, stuck people only make choices centered around their obsessions and compulsions. If it's cocaine, all choices revolve around getting more. If it's a sexual compulsion, all choices are made in light of how to hop in bed one more time—as soon as possible. If it's a food problem, all of life revolves around the menus for the basic three meals plus snacks and a binge time. All of life's choices are colored by their stuckness.

Second, stuck people tend to make few choices for themselves. Stuck people allow others to make decisions for them. They coast along unwilling to make the tough decisions in life. They either search for someone to enable them to stay stuck—those who offer choices agreeable to the stuckee—or they make no choice at all. But no choice is a choice to remain stuck. In either case, decision making by others or making no choice at all, a choice toward destruction has been made!

Growing yourself up all over again requires that you re-enter the process of becoming by making choices. *Choosing* is one of the three most significant acts that makes you human. Wise choices enable you to grow up. Foolish choices, others' choices, and no choices force you only to grow old.

Growth Step #2:
How to Re-Enter the Process of Relating

To re-enter the process of relating is to re-enter relationships. Fractured and fragmented families are overwhelming proof of how tough it is to win in relationships. Our relationships aren't working because we are missing a primary ingredient. We are missing the second of the most significant acts that makes persons human. It's *caring*. Caring and being cared for are channels for energy flow. No quality life can be developed without it.

The growth step of re-entering the process of relating is central to the other two steps. Becoming needs the relating to operate. Achieving needs the relating to keep in balance. Becoming and achieving cannot function in a vacuum. In other words, you cannot live your life successfully in a vacuum.

Since life cannot happen in a vacuum, neither can the recovery process. Stuck people, attempting to start over, often return to being stuck because of wrong relationships or no relationships. Recovery will not happen without being plugged into people. When plugged into people, three factors can emerge from the relationships. These three factors, necessary for healthy relationships, are: appreciation, accountability, and action.

Appreciation Factor: Who Cares Enough to Encourage?

An old hunter took his new retriever out early one morning to test him out. The old man shot his first bird, and the dog immediately darted after it. When the dog reached the water, he walked on top of the water, picked up the dead bird, returned on top of the water, and brought the bird back to his master. The old hunter rubbed his eyes in disbelief but decided

153

it really didn't happen. He set himself up to shoot again. Again he shot a bird, and again the dog retrieved the bird by walking on top of the water. The old hunter was amazed at his dog's behavior.

The old hunter wanted to show off his wonderful hunting dog to his best friend. So he invited him to go out hunting early the next morning. His friend got the first shot and hit a bird. The dog walked on top of the water, picked up the dead bird, returned on top of the water, and brought the bird back to his master. The old hunter said, "Do you notice anything different about my new dog?" His friend nonchalantly replied, "No, looks like just another bird dog to me."

They set up for a shot at their next victim. This time the old hunter shot the bird out of the sky. Again, his remarkable dog walked on top of the water and retrieved the bird. The old hunter asked again, "Are you sure you don't see anything different about my new dog?" His friend thought a moment and said, "Why, yes, that dog can't swim!"

Appreciation is the first critical factor in a relationship. We don't need people who always tell us what is wrong with us. We need people who will appreciate what is right with us. We must be in a relationship where we are appreciated. We need positive strokes, someone who cares about us. It's the warm fuzzies that motivate positive behavior. We all need them.

We live in a world in which people spend too much time communicating what's wrong. What we need is to be encouraged and stroked in what's right. This can't be to the point of denying the wrong and the bad, but the positive strokes of appreciation are desperately needed.

Accountability Factor: Who Cares Enough to Confront?

A middle-aged woman made her way into an apartment building to the twelfth floor. As she arrived at her intended destination, she rang the doorbell impatiently. The door opened mysteriously, and she was welcomed by the smell of incense and smoke. She entered and was greeted by a slightly dressed young girl who announced her presence with the sounding of a huge gong. With this the young girl said, "Do you wish to see the all-knowing, all-powerful, the wonderful one, Maharishi Narru?"

"Yeah," the woman said. "Tell Sheldon his mother is here!"

Accountability is the second critical factor in a relationship. There's nothing like the loving accountability of a mother. Nothing like it, except for the loving accountability of true friends plugged into caring relationships.

Accountability keeps us true to who we want to be and how we truly want to live. Accountability means that someone cares enough to hold me to my commitments. When I make commitments, I need to be plugged into people who will help me be responsible enough to keep them. It's not being responsible *for* me, but responsible *to* me.

Accountability also means caring enough to confront me when I am off-track. It's constructive criticism bathed in genuine appreciation. Destructive confrontation is a criticism with no intention of supporting the suggested change. Constructive confrontation is a criticism in which the one who confronts is willing to personally pitch in and support the suggested change.

Action Factor: Who Cares Enough to Follow Through?

A rabbit being chased by a dog through the countryside was observed by a crowd enjoying a family picnic. They cheered for the rabbit as he swiftly hopped from side to side, masterfully eluding his attacker. Then the rabbit pulled away from the dog a great distance, looked at the crowd and said, "I appreciate your encouragement, but shoot the dog!"

Action is the third critical factor in a relationship. It is the final ingredient necessary for healthy, caring relationships. We need people in our lives who are willing not just to say, "Hey, I'm your friend; you can count on me," but to act those words out and shoot the dog. This is the action factor within caring relationships.

Growth Step #3:
How to Re-Enter the Process of Achieving

Re-entering the process of achieving is re-entering responsibility. It's the responsibility to create, to make something meaningful out of your life. It's the weaving of your abilities (no matter how small) and your energies (no matter how weak) into a life fabric that has significance. Instead of coasting through life watching what happens, you must make life happen.

In addition to creating life with meaning, it is necessary to create a mission for your life. Mission and meaning go hand in hand. Search for your mission. If nothing else, do good and stop the bad! There is a critical need for each inhabitant of the world to put something back into life. Society needs it, and each individual has a need to give it!

Growing up all over again means re-entry into:

> process of becoming—learning to *choose*
> process of relating—learning to *care*
> process of achieving—learning to *create*

Growing yourself up all over again is essential as you pull yourself together in the recovery process. Don't just grow old, grow up.

But wait a minute. There's one serious problem. You can commit yourself to growing up all over again, but if you don't talk your mind into going along with it, your commitment will fizzle out!

Your Built-In Computer

Your mind is the computer control center of everything that's you. It's "the brains of your outfit." The mind, composed of ten billion, billion working parts, has enough storage capacity to accept ten new facts every second. Scientists have conservatively estimated that the human mind can store an amount of information equivalent to one hundred trillion words and that all of us use but a tiny fraction of this storage space. What you carry around with you in your head is a powerful instrument.[1]

If you're going to grow yourself up all over again, you must

---

1. Wayne Dyer, *Your Erroneous Zones* (New York: Funk and Wagnalls, 1976), p. 20.

take control of your mind. As you think, you are. As you think, you feel. As you think, you behave.

In addition to being a control center, your mind is also a giant video recorder. It has efficiently recorded everything you've ever said, heard, seen, felt, and done. Through hypnosis, a person can be taken back through life all the way to childhood. If you're asked to write your name the way you did at age sixteen, you'll write it just the way your mind recorded it when you were sixteen. If asked to write your name the way you did at seven, you'll print it exactly the way your mind recorded it at seven. The operating power of the mind is truly phenomenal.

What you put into a computer is what comes out, and the same is true for your mind. If you store negative information in your mind, negatives must come out. Garbage in, garbage out. It's like the sowing-and-reaping principle. Once the seed thought (positive or negative) has been sown, the feelings and actions which are reaped from it will be the same as the seed.

Your Brain: Use It or Lose It

Stuck people who want to start over by growing up must use their brains or risk losing everything. Humanity has a universal disease—making commitments without follow-through. We are committed but not truly involved. We are committed to family, but we don't do what we know we ought to be doing. We are committed to growing up all over again, but we don't follow through with the personal involvement. It is like the kamikaze pilot who made thirty-three missions. He was committed but not involved. Only our brains can translate commitment into action.

So how do you use your brain? Well, if you want to grow up healthy, you must feed your mind selectively. Selective feeding of the mind is called meditation. The most popular form of meditation today is "emptying" your mind (risky for most of us), but true meditation cannot occur in a vacuum. True meditation feeds your mind.

I must warn you that meditation is the most difficult activity I know of, yet I know of no other activity that is more life changing. Meditation will widen your perspective on you, your relationships, and your future as well as give you the follow-through necessary for recovery. Meditation is programming your mind for growth.

Many years ago I became hooked on meditation. I'd heard a man speak on the subject, and I decided to try it. There was one particular area of my personality that I really wanted to change, and that was my nasty habit of going berserk when anyone messed with my car. My motto was, "You mess with my car (scratch, nick, dent, or break), I'll mess with you!" The speaker had suggested that, along with meditating, an individual could find great freedom over menacing irritations in life. He suggested giving over to God the ownership of everything that seemed to be the cause of these irritations.

In response to that lecture I dove into meditation. I learned to meditate on principles from good literature. My first principle was from the Bible where it says, "Count it all joy when you fall into various trials, knowing that the testing of your faith produces patience." This simply means that when trials come in against you, be glad about it because you are going to learn some very good things about life. It is finding the handle to turn your trials and tragedies into triumph. For the life of me, I don't know why I chose this of all principles to begin with!

At the beginning of my meditation program, I also gave over the ownership of my car to God, because it definitely was the greatest cause of irritation in my life. It was a new car, a beautiful blue Buick Skylark. No scratches, nicks, dents, or breakages. I thought, "If He wants to scratch, nick, dent, or break His car, that's His business. I'm not going to worry about it!"

Various Trial #1: Attacked from the Left

We drove "God's" car over to the Los Angeles International Airport to pick up some friends. There we were, still parked, all packed up and ready to start the car, when tragedy looked me straight in the eye. A red Corvette started backing up toward my door. It really didn't bother me. Nobody in a nice, new red Corvette would even consider backing into my door. And then, while still in reverse, the driver gunned it! He backed up into my door and made an incredible indentation.

Rage rose up in my body. I was about to go berserk! Just

before I blew, a sign appeared in my mind's eye: "Count it all joy when you fall into various trials, knowing that the testing of your faith produces patience!" And it was signed, God. I had very little choice. I made my way out of the car, through the passenger side for obvious reasons. The man who hit me proceeded to cuss me as if it were my fault. I explained to him, "I didn't have the car running. And if it had been running, my car only goes forward and backward, not sideways." He couldn't seem to understand that, and he took off in a huff. No insurance, no license, no license plates, no police officer, no nothing to help me find justice. And there sat God's car with a very large indentation on the left front door.

Various Trial #2: Attacked from the Right

About ten days later we went camping up the West Coast with another couple. At our first campsite, tragedy faced me again, eyeball to eyeball. My buddy was standing by the passenger side door, pulling down the tent and grill, but he didn't have a good hold on the grill. The grill came down across the beautiful blue paint on the door and created an interesting, yet gross design with its scratches and scrapes. I was standing only fifteen feet behind him at the time. As I made my natural move toward berserkness, that crazy sign appeared in my mind's eye again: "Count it all joy when you fall into various trials. . . ." I asked myself, "Is this a various trial?" It was! I then said, "Don't worry about it, Dick." Then I turned around to see if I really said that, because that wasn't normal for me.

Well, I liked what was happening to me. Some things were changing in my life that needed to be changed. I wasn't losing control anymore. That was terrific because it was rough being known as the person who messed up people's bodies after they messed up my car.

Various Trial #3: Attacked from the Rear

Only a few weeks later we were back in school in Dallas. On the way to school one morning, I was going down a one-way street. In the right lane was another car that wanted to make a left-hand turn but would have to go through me to do it. And he did! He made his left-hand turn, hit my right back fender, and turned me completely around in the middle of the street. Rage and terror began to move through my body, and my berserk state was just around the corner. I thought I had learned this lesson earlier. But there I was again, sitting repeating this class all over again, Remedial Self-Control 101. All of a sudden that sign from my meditation appeared again, and I was able to channel my anger into compassion for the other driver. He was an old man who was really scared and shaken up, and I was able to offer him help.

Various Trial #4: Attacked from the Front

That same day I was making my way to downtown Dallas from north of the city. In order to go from north to south, I had to take the central expressway. Now, if you have ever been to Dallas, you know that there are no entrances onto the central expressway. Chutes, maybe. Launching pads, possibly. But no entrances. So there I was, getting ready to launch out onto central with only one car in front of me. It was drizzling that afternoon, which made the streets exceptionally slippery.

The car in front of me was driven by a young student from Thailand. When he accelerated for launching, his wheels began spinning. This scared him so that he stopped at the end of the chute. Well, I didn't know that. I was looking back at the cars on the freeway, waiting for a chance to safely launch into the traffic flow. I had seen the car in front of me take off, and by the time I got my chance he should have been well on his way downtown. So, with my head looking back, I gunned it for the launch. I came to an abrupt stop when I rammed into the back of his car. My hood flew up, so I didn't know what in the world I had hit. All I could see was my blue hood.

I got out of my car only to see the guy from Thailand holding his neck and saying some very angry things in Thai. Later the police arrived. The first thing the officer said to me was, "Is this your car?" (I didn't have the guts to say, "No, it's actually God's car!" I knew they would give me the breath test for sure.) The officer helped me tie down my hood and fasten it with wire.

We lived in a fourth-story apartment, so when I got home I parked the car for my wife to get a total view of the latest damage. There were the indentation in the left door, the unusual design on the right door, the wrinkle in the right back fender, and the new bow in the hood. As I walked into the apartment my wife asked, "Why aren't you at your appointment?" I said, "Take a look outside." She looked at God's car and observed, "You are still learning some things, aren't you?"

Overhauling Your Mind

Selective meditation is the entire overhauling process of the mind. It demands that you search and sift out all of the information available to you. The overhauling process is preparatory work for "psychological digestion." The mind food you order for meditation will determine the kinds of digestion you'll experience. If you order junk food for your mind, you may experience problems in your psychological digestion. Junk food is the normal diet for the world of the stuck.

Your menu consists of input from the movies, books, TV, radio, and relationships that feeds into your mind-computer daily. You must screen out that which is harmful and feed on that which is most nutritious.

After ordering your mind food, you must bite into it. I always look for principles of life that can be applied from life stories, teachers, or biblical sections. Good material has never been my problem, but application of it is another story. Unless I am able to chew up my bite-sized chunks of principles for a period of time, they're almost impossible to apply. Like most people, I rationalize when I do things wrong by saying, "I didn't know" or "I forgot." The chewing process is extremely important because the more you think about your mind food, the deeper it sinks into your psyche. Writing out your mind-food menu on a three by five index card can be helpful in meditating. You can put it on your desk, fasten it to the refrigerator door, or carry it with you so you can keep chewing on the principles throughout the week. Finally, you must swallow them. Swallowing is the process of applying the principles of life to your life situations, of making wise choices in line with the principles you have chosen.

No matter how you meditate, do it. Meditation is the overhauling process of the mind. Without it, your recovery could be just another temporary hype. Remember: If you decide to go for recovery, you must talk your mind into going along with you or you won't make it!

Recovery:
Pulling Yourself Together

One evening an elderly couple sat down before their television set for a relaxing evening of viewing. As the couple sat there watching, the woman began to think of times past. She looked over at her husband Orville and asked, "Orville, do you remember when we were first married, and how you would reach over and hold my hand while we watched television?"

Orville looked up at her and said, "I sure do." He then reached over and held her hand.

A few minutes later, she questioned him again. "Orville, do you remember when you used to put your arm around me when we watched television?"

Orville said that he did, and he reached over and gently put his arm around his wife.

A few minutes later, the wife looked up at Orville and questioned him once again. "But, Orville, do you remember when we used to watch television and you would bite me on the back of the neck?"

Orville immediately rose to his feet and walked toward the door. His wife looked startled and asked, "Orville, where are you going?"

He turned around and told her, "I'm going to get my teeth!"

Orville knew that if he was going to do a job he needed the proper equipment. The same principle applies to recovery. You need the right equipment or tools if recovery is to be a lasting, ongoing process.

Hung Up on the Cause

In recovery, people often get hung up on the cause of the problem rather than doing something about the problem. People search, depending on their profession or perspective, for a spiritual or mental or emotional cause of the problem. Often this search is nothing more than an attempt to place the blame or reinforce a biased or judgmental opinion. Discovering the source or cause has little to do with recovery.

Consider an alcoholic who has been drinking for twenty years. Let us say that the alcoholic is a male and he seeks help from a psychiatrist. The psychiatrist, in attempting to help the alcoholic, tries to explore the reason he began drinking twenty years ago. This might be done in an attempt to discover some unresolved developmental conflict. The desired result would be for the alcoholic to discover the unresolved conflict, work through it, resolve it, and eradicate the need to drink. But this is a futile effort. Why a person started drinking twenty years ago has nothing to do with why that person would be drinking twenty years later. In those twenty years there might have been deaths, divorces, losses of jobs, or many other things more traumatic than that same conflict in the distant past. In addition, after twenty years of heavy drinking, the primary reason for drinking may be pure and simple addiction. The man's body may have adapted to the chemical, and he may become ill when the drinking is stopped. A case could be made that the main reason for his drinking is survival.

The wise psychiatrist, and there are many, first looks to the methods of how to stop drinking long before any consideration is given to why the drinking started. The method of stopping fits into the entire system designed for the recovery of the whole individual. The system does not focus on any one area, such as physical or mental. It encompasses every area of the person's life.

Hung Up on Stopping

Another mistake in recovery, just as futile as looking only for the source, is attempting simply to stop the problem. Again, in the case of the alcoholic, stopping the drinking is not the goal. The goal is the recovery of the whole person. The whole person involves physical, mental, emotional, social, and spiritual components. Stopping drinking has nothing to do with whether or not a person is able to grow spiritually. To grow in the spiritual dimension the individual must first stop drinking, but the actual growth process will involve much, much more.

Taking limited action is another common mistake. Whether someone has a predisposition to gain weight or is obsessed with sexual perversions due to some childhood trauma, if that person is going to do something about the problem, the action taken cannot be one-dimensional. It cannot involve only one aspect of the person's life. Focusing on one area only serves to delay total recovery. The person is paralyzed further in a mixture of will power and good intentions that produces only temporary results. Liberation from the problem comes from a total recovery system.

The components of recovery are the same for all problems. There may be some unique feature of treatment for some problems that is not necessary for others, but the basic elements are the same. Quick fixes and instant cures have nothing to do with recovery. Recovery is a process that occurs over time. And it never ends. It is not a point that a person reaches. It is an ongoing growth process that builds on the growth of yesterday. The simplest definition for recovery is growth. And that growth encompasses every area of the person's life.

Physical Recovery: In Search of a New Body

The first area to consider in the recovery process is physical or physiological recovery. Physiological recovery involves all of the growth elements that pertain to the physical body. It is the most concrete area and forms a foundation on which the other recovery components are built.

Detoxification, exercise, relaxation, and nutrition combine to form the physiological component of the recovery system. When the physical component is developed, the other components in the recovery system are much easier and stable. If a person wants to get unstuck and start over, the place to begin is with the body.

Clean Up

Detoxification is an important first step in physical recovery. If detoxification is not handled properly for the addicted person, relapse will be instant. Detoxification for the addicted individual involves controlled withdrawal from the addictive chemical. An alcoholic might be detoxified with the use of Valium. The amount of Valium is stepped down in a controlled system until the addict is no longer ingesting any chemicals. Other chemicals are used to detoxify from other substances. Catapress is used for heroin addicts. The purpose of the use of the chemicals in detoxification from other chemicals is to control an unpredictable situation. For years an alcoholic may repeatedly attempt alone to stop drinking, and then on one last attempt, do it alone and die from withdrawal. It is important that the detoxification process be controlled and handled professionally in a treatment center. When it is accomplished without chemicals, called social detox, it must be handled by experienced individuals who can respond appropriately if the person does go into a severe withdrawal.

When a person stops taking an addictive chemical, the detoxification process is not over. It involves much more. True detoxification involves freeing the body from impurities that have built up over the years. Many different methods are used to achieve the flushing of impurities. They range from coffee enemas to repeated saunas and the ingestion of certain substances that cling to impurities and allow them to be flushed from the system. This further step in the detoxification process can be valuable, especially for those who have bombarded their system with junk foods and a highly processed diet. The freer the body is from chemicals and impurities, the better.

Work Out

Physical recovery also involves an exercise program. The level of exercise will vary from person to person, depending on the overall condition of the body. This is best assessed by a physician. In the early stages of recovery it is vital that at least once each day the person exercises to the point of perspiring. This perspiration will assist in the detoxification of the system. Pores will be unclogged, and impurities will be flooded out of the body through perspiration.

Exercise has other added benefits. It is the most natural form of stimulation. When the body starts to move, the mind eventually catches up and begins to move also. Many depressed people have begun the process of recovery by getting out of bed, starting to take walks, and eventually jogging or swimming. Studies have shown that exercise is an effective treatment in alleviating depression and establishing emotional stability. The person who is used to getting a high or a rush from food, drink, drugs, purchases, gambling, pornography, or whatever the source of being hooked will find that exercise can provide the same type of relief—except that exercise is beneficial rather than destructive. And the price is reasonable.

Exercise is also a natural way to get rid of tension. Nothing is more helpful in the day to day management of stress than regular exercise. When tension mounts or anger flares into a rage, when a person feels as if the limit has been reached and no more stress can be tolerated, a brisk walk, run, or swim can soothe the emotions and return the person to a manageable state. Rather than allowing pressure and stress to build up, a two- or three-minute walk several times a day can assist a person in regaining perspective and keep the build-up of stress to a minimum. Whether it is stimulation or relaxation, exercise can provide needed relief. It is an inexpensive means of getting out of a mood and on the move. Recovery is not complete without exercise.

Exercise also should be considered as a healthy means of developing family involvement and interaction. A man in treatment for alcoholism and compulsive gambling missed this point when he set out to include exercise in his recovery program. The man was greatly depressed, grieved, and in need of his family's support after the sudden death of his mother. He was convinced that exercise should be a big part of his recovery.

The man lived close to a bay and he purchased a kayak so he could row out on the bay in the morning and evening. But his exercise was soon out of perspective. He reached a point where he was rowing two hours in the morning and three hours in the evening. It became a ritual for him, and he was proud of both his body and the distance he could row. All of this surfaced when his wife spoke up about her loneliness and anger over her husband's recovery program. She complained that he actually spent more time on his "little rowboat" than he had spent gambling or drinking. She wanted to know where the family fit into the program.

The man had used the exercise as a means of escape rather than as a way of solidifying his recovery. His depression and grief motivated his flight from relationships. His recovery really began when he replaced some of the time with his paddle with some quality time with his family. Exercise, though important, must be kept in perspective.

Another man, however, understood the benefits of exercise and how it could bring a disjointed family together again. The family had been through many disasters. The mother was a classic workaholic. She was a real estate agent who never stopped studying listings, locating new properties, or touring prospective clients. The father had a regular nine-to-five job, but the mother was never off work. She had made thousands of dollars from her efforts but lost even more from poor investments. She also had lost a son in Vietnam. She had never resolved his death, and anger continued to pull her down into depression after depression. One of the daughters had become pregnant and had an abortion at age fifteen and since then had done poorly in school. The entire family was in pain, and the father finally sought help.

The family counselor suggested to the father that he try to get the family involved together in a number of ways. One was church, the other was exercise. So Dad went home and called a family meeting. He requested at the meeting that he be given one night of the week by the mother and two daughters for a family event. Reluctantly they worked out that on every Monday night the family was the priority. The first Monday the father took everyone down to the sporting goods store and bought tennis racquets and clothes. The next week he hired a tennis instructor to give the family the first of eight lessons.

They religiously kept their Monday nights open for tennis night. It was filled with laughter and fun and provided the family with a point of reference. It was something they all had in common and could talk about during the week. The tennis sessions also were great exercise for Mom. Her depressions became less and less severe. In addition, she began to open up more to her family. She eventually was able to share her hurt and resentment and how so many expectations had been lost with the death of her son. Exercise had been the central point at which the family members, especially Mom, began to move again. It was the vital link between stuck and starting over.

Tennis revolutionized a family in the process of recovery. Later, the family started jogging together in the mornings. Together. That's the component that makes a family a family rather than a collection of people. When physical recovery is at its best, it involves exercise with other people. It becomes an excuse to get involved.

Calm Down

Physical recovery also involves relaxation. Relaxation is scheduled time outs for the body and mind to rest and relax. Relapse is often a result of a person's becoming so busy that there is no time to relax and reflect on life. Relaxation is a time to block out everything and let nothing interfere or interrupt. Paying attention to the body, especially to breathing, assists in the relaxation process. Many techniques can be used, but the most beneficial is to schedule ten or fifteen minutes a day for the purpose of relaxing. Prayer can be utilized during this time of stopping and re-energizing. Relaxation allows the body's ability to heal itself to function at its best. Solid recovery involves a regular shutdown of the outside world for a time of refreshing relaxation. When the world seems out of control, structured times of relaxation allow a person to regain control and grow in the recovery process.

Eat It Up—Properly

The physical component in recovery also involves nutrition. Strength and stability will not come from eating junk. Food can be used to keep the body clean and healthy as well as to control mood swings. Nutrition adds to the stability factor of recovery.

Proper foods aid in rebuilding damaged tissues, and they also promote growth of the whole person.

The recovery diet is the opposite from the standard American diet. It is low in fat, sugar, caffeine, chemicals, and junk foods. It is high in complex carbohydrates, whole grain foods, vegetables, but limited in protein. When good food replaces junk food, blood sugar levels stabilize and mood swings decrease. The person finds more sustained energy and a decrease in periods of frantic nervousness.

Nutrition in recovery involves learning how to eat as well as what to eat. The custom of eating three large meals a day, for instance, may best be replaced by eating three smaller meals and three small nutritious snacks. Evidence from thousands of people in recovery points to this way of eating as preferable because it provides longer sustained energy and fewer mood swings, headaches, and tension. It prevents the roller coaster effect of a high blood sugar level followed by a distinct drop. This drop in blood sugar often leads to a craving sensation. This nonspecific craving often leads the person to relapse and repeat the very act that needs to be eliminated. Many nutritionists think that frequent meals, full of nutritious whole, non-processed foods, allow the body to mend itself and the mind to function with stability.

Mental Recovery: In Search of a New Mind

Mental recovery refers to the thinking processes of the brain rather than the emotional aspects of the mind. Mental recovery allows a person to regain judgment, make positive decisions, and communicate effectively. Mental recovery is based on an individual's ability to alter his or her thinking process. Built upon a strong physical recovery, mental recovery is the key to emotional healing as well.

Think Positive

The mind must be fed new, accurate information about the problem and the rest of how life works. When trapped or stuck, people tend to believe and accept only the information that supports the denial that has been built around the problem. For instance, a man who is a rapist will latch onto articles and books that support the inability of the rapist to change the destructive behavior. If a study points to this perversion as beyond rehabilitation, or that the problem actually surfaces or develops during teen years, he will hold onto the information and allow himself to feel a sense of hopelessness and complacency. Information that supports the need to accept responsibility and receive help, stories of complete recoveries from sexual perversions and cases of violence are disregarded. Recovery of the mind utilizes information that points toward the hope of change rather than the despair of helplessness.

Information helpful in alerting the thinking process comes in many forms. Probably the best source is hearing someone speak who has recovered from the same or a similar problem. This reinforces that others have had problems, even worse in intensity, and have been able to overcome them. In addition, it provides good, common-sense help on how to put together and maintain a solid recovery plan. It moves a person away from feeling alone and hopeless to knowing that there is hope and that others have built a new life on that hope. Alcoholics Anonymous holds regular Speaker Meetings where recovering alcoholics relate how it was, what happened, and how it is today. Many speakers are inspirational, but more importantly, they reinforce the recovery process with information that changes the thinking process.

Lectures, tapes, and books about problems and recovery help people refocus mentally. Years of negative input must be reversed. The mind is best saturated with information from every source available. As the facts begin to sink into a person's conscious thinking, attitudes develop about life and self-change for the better. In formalized treatment, clients and patients are involved in many sessions to build solid attitudes for recovery. Lectures are reinforced with discussion groups. Reading assignments are augmented with cassette tapes. All of this is designed to assist in a change of thinking and in the development of positive attitudes. Recovery is impossible without new information to replace the old.

Just as it is important to acquire new, positive information, it is important to discard old, negative information. Media, such as television or movies, that can reinforce old attitudes must be discontinued. A woman named Nancy was in an eating disorder unit due to an extreme case of obesity. She had a miserable marriage and felt that food was the only source of pleasure in her life. Her misery was magnified by what she watched on television every day. Nancy not only was stuck on food but also was hooked on soap operas. Day after day she watched women involved in exciting affairs. She also saw betrayal, death, helplessness, and depression. She spent her days saturating her mind with negative thoughts while she filled her body with junk. Finally she sought help, entered treatment, and lost sixty pounds.

When she left treatment she was full of optimism and hope for a new life. But her best intentions were diluted by an old habit. She returned to the soap operas. She started watching at 12:00 and by 4:00 she was eating out of control again. A more realistic appraisal of the situation would have pointed out the need to discontinue the soap operas and their negative influence if the weight was going to stay off. But once again she found herself trapped. She gained back the sixty pounds before she decided she could reverse her relapse.

Nancy sold her television set. She refused to have it sitting in the house tempting her. She started reading and filling the time with good books and magazines. She bought a small cassette tape player and listened to tapes while she worked around the house. It revolutionized the way she thought and her ability to communicate her ideas with other people. Her thoughts and her attitudes complemented her intentions to change her life.

A wise friend recommended something that helped her mental recovery. The friend suggested that she keep a journal to be filled with facts, concepts, quotes, and principles that were positive and insightful. Nancy bought a small notebook and began to journalize any information that she felt was helpful. She wrote down anything that reinforced the recovery concepts that had helped her lose weight. These basic truths she compiled formed her own recovery manual. When she had a bad day or felt depressed, she would refer to the meaningful concepts she had written. She continued her weight loss, and while losing the weight she gained a new mind. She was able to communicate what she knew and became an excellent writer.

She guarded herself from the negative influences that could precipitate another relapse. Her recovery was solid because she changed what went into her mind and learned to communicate what was in her mind.

My Friend, My Enemy

The other area of mental recovery that often causes a problem is friends and acquaintances. It is frustrating to work on thinking differently only to have a "friend" tear down what was believed to be true. The fact is, a lot of people unconsciously are destructive to the people they call friends. One of the easiest forms of destruction is to question or argue about everything that the recovering persons find helpful. The know-it-all friends question everything new rather than support change. Friends who badger with "How do you know?" or "Who told you that?" or "Where is the proof?" can sap the positive energy away from the person struggling for a better life. These people must be avoided. Their input is detrimental to mental recovery.

In summary, the mind and the thinking process are vital to solid recovery. An attempt must be made to absorb information that can change thoughts and attitudes. Books, movies, television programs, or friends that reinforce old thoughts or attitudes must be avoided. Mental recovery requires support from people as well as media. And on top of it is established emotional recovery. But the feelings will not heal unless the brain thinks and makes decisions based on new information about life and recovery.

Emotional Recovery: In Search of Lost Feelings

Emotional recovery is built upon the strengths of both physical and mental components. Emotions are never stabilized when the nervous system is affected by caffeine, nicotine, sugar, or any other substance that a person may be sensitive to. In addition, what people think about or tell themselves forms the feelings and emotions. A confused mind leads to confused emotions. If feelings are to be manageable, the body and mind must work together to accomplish it.

173

Emotional recovery is commonly delayed because it can be painful. Searching for suppressed feelings and struggling to express them are not easy or fun. Introspection is an appropriate part of emotional recovery. It is the time to be still while exploring and expressing the feelings that make life uncomfortable. Introspection balances the movement forward.

People are relieved to find that they do not have to go through life as stoics. Knowing that they do not have to conceal their feelings behind an emotional stone wall adds a freedom not experienced before. People do not get well when emotions are hidden. Cancer patients get sicker when they try to hide anger and fear. Hiding emotions just forms a barrier that prevents the fullness of life from being felt. The words in the song title "You Are Only as Sick as Your Secrets" are true. What people hide, especially in the area of feelings, only produces needless pain and desperation.

You Can't Go It Alone

Emotional recovery cannot occur alone. It must be done in relationships with others who are helpful and supportive. It is best accomplished in a group setting that might be a recovery group, a self-help group, or a growth group. Whatever its name, there is great power within a group. In groups where people share problems, discuss feelings, and provide support, group members are able to grow emotionally. Members learn to accept others, their differences and contrasting approaches to problems. They learn to listen as others share in the struggles of recovery. But most importantly, they learn to express authentic thoughts and emotions. The group is able to confront the facade and challenge each member to be real.

The battle cry of the stuck person is always, "I can do it alone!" It is an effort to convince themselves as well as others that everything will be better because of the motivation to change. But alone, the emotional growth needed in recovery does not happen. That is why too many people may stop drinking or stealing or practicing some sexual perversion but they never start growing. The person out there still struggling alone, still disconnected from people and relationships, will remain emotionally immature. In various types of treatment it is common to hear people describe themselves at age forty-five as emotionally still at age sixteen. They talk of how the emotional development came to a standstill at the point when the drinking, drugging, gambling, spending, or "whatever" began. Rather than face an uncomfortable feeling and resolve it, they talk of running to that "whatever" for instant relief. The group setting is designed to reverse that habit or process and allow the missing emotional development to occur. Thousands in recovery attest to the fact that the group is where emotional recovery takes place. Thousands of others still struggling alone are also proof of the importance of the group.

The group fosters the accountability factor from one individual to another. Accountability as a group dynamic goes beyond the standard supportive relationship. The dimension of confrontation it provides stimulates emotional growth and maturity. It is easy for a group to slip into a rut in which everyone expresses feelings and talks about how everything is going. But when accountability is added to that group, the members are challenged to take action. If someone is depressed, the group might suggest that the person agree to be out of bed each morning by 8:00 A.M. and take a brisk walk before doing anything else. The accountability factor motivates the depressed person because he or she knows a report must be given to the group the next week. The group will hold the person accountable to complete the assignment and report on the effects of that assignment. The group will follow up with the person in a supportive and caring manner but will also be confrontive if the person does not complete the task. All of this reinforces the person's ability to develop self-accountability. When the group is not around, the individual is accountable to himself or herself for the consequences of actions or inactions. This then continues the process of maturity and emotional recovery.

By the time a person has progressed through the cycle of destruction and is ready to recover, almost every relationship in which there was accountability has been destroyed. Often a problem gets worse faster because of this lack. Frequently, highly placed, powerful men and women have fallen hard because no one was around to say what needed to be said or to assist them in getting back on track. Since lack of accountability compounds problems, it is vital to have it when recovery begins. Beyond any kind of group accountability in recovery, a one-to-one personal level of accountability is needed. Many self-help groups encourage members to acquire a sponsor who is valuable to a person's recovery and growth. The sponsor is often the only person who can say, "Shut up and listen!" when it is needed most.

Confrontation of ongoing denial is a priority. After people have started the recovery process and things begin to feel better, there is a tendency for denial to grow. The denial is subtle, but it comes in the form of "Well, the problem really is not that bad yet," or "I'm really not as bad as some of these other people." In a group, as in any accountable relationship, this emerging denial can be confronted before it reaches a deadly stage. When people again start to deny their condition, growth stops and recovery stops. Emotionally the person begins to revert to old feelings that were and will be destructive again. Relationships, whether group or individual, are essential in confronting the ongoing denial that subtly creeps in to destroy progress.

Confrontation through accountability forces every person to look inside at the hidden, isolated self that lies buried beneath the facades of deception. Many people are afraid to uncover the real self because it is full of both strengths and weaknesses. Emotional recovery gradually unveils the real person hidden beneath obsessions, compulsions, and compensations. Emotional recovery is the discovery of authenticity.

Authentic people, saturated with the reality of who they are, are rare. Authenticity and emotional maturity develop as a person continues to accept weaknesses as reality yet proceeds to build upon strengths. Again, a group of supportive people is the best facilitator of this genuine growth and recovery. Each gathering together eats away at the isolation of the real person. Weaknesses are supported and strengths reinforced until a person is able to grasp and live comfortably with no more or no less than who he or she really is. Breaking through to that unique human being inside who so desperately wants to be expressed is the result of emotional recovery. The genuine person is able to accept self, identify real feelings, and express these feelings appropriately. When this occurs, the person can move out into the next realm of recovery, the social dimension.

Social Recovery: In Search of Healthy Relationships

How can a person be comfortable with others if that person is uncomfortable with himself or herself? It cannot be done. That is why emotional recovery is essential before a person can recover socially. Too often, wounded and struggling people in recovery rush out into the world long before they have developed emotional strength. The result is intense discomfort, overwhelming feelings of inferiority, and a sense of being out of place. Recovery must be gradual at first. It cannot develop until internal emotional growth has been achieved to sustain it. Frequently those who fail in a social context need to start over and complete the emotional growth that was neglected.

Social recovery refers to getting things together in relation to other people. Humans are social creatures. In the social dimension varying degrees of relationships are played out, developed, and nurtured. Social recovery involves regaining perspective of those relationships and understanding how and where they will be enhanced or diminished. At times the herd instinct runs rampant. An individual loses touch with the real self or never develops because of the drive to be a part of the crowd. This drive is motivated by loneliness. In an effort to cure the loneliness, the lonely person attempts to latch onto the crowd or the herd and then finds that the feelings of alienation are still there. To resolve the conflict, a person must consider who is in the crowd and where the crowd is going. Aimlessly wandering in and out of groups, continuing to feel isolated and lonely, is the opposite of social recovery.

Taking Time for a Social Inventory

In the initial stages of social recovery, it is helpful to do a social inventory to determine what areas are healthy and where some social construction would be helpful. The following are some areas to cover in the inventory:

1. With whom am I spending the most time?
2. What do we do when we are together?
3. Do I feel like our being together has been healthy or does it leave me feeling somewhat empty?

4. What do I do with my family?
5. How much time do I give to activities of leisure with my family?
6. What groups outside the family am I involved in?
7. Is my association with outside groups constructive with regard to my recovery?
8. Who is consistently the most supportive person in my life?
9. Do I spend enough time with that supportive person?
10. Who always brings out the worst in me?
11. How often do I get trapped into spending time with that person?
12. Who are the people I have wanted to get to know but have failed to make an effort?
13. What are some groups that I could become a part of?
14. Where is the unhealthiest place I go?
15. What can I do to substitute for the time spent there?
16. Who seems interested in sharing a part of what I do, think, and feel?
17. What could I do to make opportunities for those caring people to share my world?
18. What defense mechanism do I throw up that prevents people from getting to know me?
19. In what situations do I find it hardest to be myself?
20. Where do I feel most comfortable with myself and those around me?

These questions can be helpful in formulating a plan for social recovery. An honest self-assessment can reveal the areas that most need change and development. An important and often painful part of that assessment is the discovery of those people who are detrimental to the recovery process. Those are the people who could be appropriately called negative social pressure.

Changing Playmates and Playgrounds

Playmates. For years, self-help and recovery groups have identified the need to "change playmates and playgrounds" as a vital link to social recovery. Some people will pretend to be sup-

portive but, because of their own insecurity, will move a recovering person toward relapse. It cannot be denied that when
an alcoholic recovers, he or she is a threat to former drinking
partners. The healthy eater is often a nuisance to unhealthy
eaters. People who are still stuck will destroy the recovery process. The destruction comes from belittling questions: "Now
what new thing are you into?" or "I wonder how long it will last
this time?" Statements like "I know you can control it better
than before; you are much stronger now" or "You know that
just a little couldn't hurt" are especially destructive when they
come from family members.

Friends and family, even the most unhealthy ones, are not to
be forsaken forever in the name of growth and recovery. But in
the initial stages of recovery, some people must be given little
access for a while. That is why it is best for certain individuals
to spend a month or two in a recovery house. The time away
allows the family to grow and adjust to a new and recovering
person. It also prevents unintentional but uncaring statements
from building up and causing greater anger and bitterness. A
time away is also an appropriate move to avoid unhealthy
friends for a while. Then, in another time under other circumstances when recovery is more secure and stable, developing
new relationships can be attempted with old friends and family
members.

Playgrounds. Changing playgrounds is another step toward
a healthy social recovery. Some places are not conducive to
growth and recovery. It is an obvious dilemma. For example,
Las Vegas is not the place for a recovering gambler to vacation.
Overeaters would best conduct meetings in places other than a
restaurant. Alcoholics who continue to work as bartenders flirt
with disaster. And afternoons in a porn shop are the beginning
of more trouble for the child molester. Certain areas must be
considered off limits if healthy social recovery is to be lasting.
The single in search of a meaningful relationship may need to
say good-bye to singles bars forever. The principle is to avoid
the unhealthy people and unhealthy places.

To balance the elimination of certain unhealthy unsocial pressure, positive social support should be developed. Those people and places that exert a positive influence should be
cultivated. Everyone needs a cheering section. People who are

accepting and always looking for the best are invaluable—not the people who are filled with great intentions, but the ones who are always there with an encouraging word when needed.

A young mother and father who lost their child in a shooting accident attribute their survival to two other couples who stood beside them through the ordeal and who carefully helped them move back into the world of friends and out of their lonely depression. The acquisition of these great personal crusaders can assist in the reemergence into relationships. Joyce Landorf calls these people "balcony people." Social recovery hinges on the elimination of negative social pressures and the active pursuit of balcony people.

Social recovery begins the process of sharing life with others rather than hiding from people who want to grow close. It is all about making decisions that are healthy and supportive of recovery rather than staying stuck in destructive relationships and situations. When someone recovers socially, he or she moves out of a totally self-centered existence and reaffirms the value of relationships. The focus eventually moves from "Who can help me?" to "How can I make a contribution?" This area of recovery leads a person to reestablish old relationships and mend past hurts. But in the beginning, social recovery cannot be rushed and must be handled delicately. The recovering person must decide that no person or place is more important than recovery. This does not mean divorce when a spouse is not supportive, but it could mean temporary separation for the sake of long-term recovery.

Social recovery is facilitated by a recovery group. Interaction between people is often strained and difficult in the early recovery stages. Establishing supportive relationships is hampered by negative attitudes that occasionally pop up and by inappropriate statements that slip out. The group provides a supportive environment where a person can rehearse for the outside world, polishing some of the rough edges of negative self-centeredness. Of all the options for positive social support and development, a recovery group is the best.

In the end, the person who does not recover socially does not recover at all. To take thoughts and feelings and share them in experiences is a major portion of life. To miss out on it is to miss life to the fullest. Recovery of the whole person must include recovering close relationships also. Social creatures need social recovery.

Spiritual Recovery: In Search of God

Recovery is never complete until a person develops the spiritual dimension. But it is a difficult dimension to discuss because of misconceptions and preconceived ideas about concepts of spiritual growth. What must be remembered is that everyone is in a different place in the journey toward spiritual growth. Those further down the path must understand the difficulty involved with spiritual recovery for those who have spent years feeling alienated from God, religious institutions, or anything that had any connection with religion. For the person who has grown and matured spiritually, the concepts presented here may appear too vague or noncommittal; for the atheist or agnostic, these principles may appear too "religious." Wherever a person is on the journey toward spiritual recovery, it is a priority to be accepting rather than judgmental toward those either in front or behind on the road toward growth and recovery.

Spiritual growth has nothing to do with religion. Those who shy away from religion need not avoid spiritual growth. Organized religion should exist to facilitate spiritual growth of groups with common beliefs. Because a religion may have lost that mission, or because a religious organization may stand in the way, does not mean that the issue of spiritual growth can be avoided. Within every religious organization there are many genuinely spiritual people. When the church or religion assists in the spiritual growth process, it is helpful for the recovering person to be a part of that church or religion.

Certain recovery groups discount the importance of church in the recovery process. But the right church for the right person can be a strong support. Old attitudes about people with problems are changing. What was once a source of alienation is now a source of help and acceptance for people with all types of problems. The problem is not religion or church; the problem is those individuals who have used the church and religion for selfish motives, even profiteering. The whole should not be

181

judged based upon a few parts. The significance of presenting problems with religion and church upon entering the area of spiritual growth lies in the association made between spirituality and religion. Even though they are separate issues, attitudes about one are deeply rooted in the other.

People often substitute "getting religious" for genuine spiritual growth. They wrap religion and the church around themselves to present an image of respectability. In search of spiritual growth, people can get trapped into a form of compensation called religiosity or religious fanaticism. Growing in order to look better has no place in the spiritual dimension. Spiritual growth, when complete, produces a congruency between what is on the inside and what is on the outside. What looks good to the outside world must be sacrificed for what produces genuine internal spiritual growth.

Spiritual growth begins with an acknowledgement of the existence of a higher power, a power greater than the individual that can greatly assist in the growth process and with personal problems. The term higher power is offensive to some who profess a strong belief in God. The question comes up, "Why call it a higher power? Why not just use the word *God?*" The answer is easily explained. Recovery is for everyone. It is for everyone from the thirteen-year-old prostitute to the sixty-three-year-old minister. Recovery concepts are applicable to those two and everyone in between. The minister most likely believes in God. The prostitute may not. But the minister may be just as stuck as the prostitute. The minister may believe there is a God but may not trust God as a higher power. The minister may only tap into his own personal power.

If God is God in a person's life, God is acknowledged as more powerful than the individual. Some people state a belief in God, but in reality they acknowledge no one or nothing as more powerful than themselves. Their ego, or will, is all-powerful, even though they may preach on the power of God. For them, recovery is only possible when they acknowledge God as a higher power.

The term *higher power* is also significant for the person who professes to be an atheist. If that person cannot in the beginning accept that God exists, then the person must acknowledge something as more powerful than the individual. The atheist may be able to accept only that the group of supportive people is the higher power. That is an acceptable place to begin the spiritual journey. But rarely does that person stick with the concept of the group or something else as a higher power. In almost every case, that person eventually is able to accept the reality of God as the higher power.

Recovery Without God would be the title of the saddest book I could write. Time and again people set themselves up as all-powerful in their own recovery and they fail. Recurring relapse is frequently the result of a person attempting recovery without God as the higher power. When spiritual growth is nonexistent, other areas of recovery deteriorate also. Those most skeptical about God and the need for spiritual growth are often the most miserable in recovery.

Spiritual recovery is the dimension that completes the recovery process. Through spiritual recovery, the value of the individual, personal relationships, and the family are restored. Freedom from guilt, anger, and fear is experienced as the person recovers spiritually. Hope returns where despair prevailed. And as an individual grows spiritually, priorities change. Life is lived from the perspective of God's wisdom and not from the limited view of momentary gratification. Through spiritual recovery, life has purpose and meaning. No longer covered by denial and other defensive barriers, the mature, genuine person emerges. It is in the area of spiritual recovery that the stuck person obtains the freedom to be real.

When spiritual recovery is combined with emotional, mental, physical, and social recovery, the whole person is able to experience all of the opportunities of life that every individual deserves to enjoy. But recovery involves discipline, and at times very painful discipline, for it to be lasting and complete. The discipline of recovering in all five areas is like the tension on a kite that enables the kite to soar above the earth. It is the discipline within the recovery system that allows freedom and hope to grow rather than diminish. All five areas must be developed in disciplined perspective to each other. One dimension can never be ignored as some other dimension becomes the focus of recovery.

Summary. Whatever the source of the problem, this recovery system is the answer for moving out of addiction and codependency and into recovery. Delay in implementing the system should never occur in an effort to search for the reasons why or the source of the problem. Recovery is available to anyone who is willing to enter the process of developing every area into a whole person. But a person cannot recover alone. And there is no reason to attempt recovery alone. Plenty of resources are available to assist the recovery process. Treatment centers, out-patient programs, counselors, and self-help programs have worked for years to help people recover. Once people develop the willingness to start over, help is available for them. Years of devastation and destruction can be resolved by reaching out to someone who can help.

Relapse: One Step Forward, Three Steps Backward

After a long and grueling week of hard work, a father, whose only intent for a Sunday afternoon was to lie down and take a nice long nap, had to overcome just one obstacle standing in the way of achieving his goal. That obstacle was his six-year-old little boy, whose only intent was to spend the afternoon playing with his father. Every time the father settled in on the living room sofa, the little boy would sneak in, pull on his dad's shirt, and beg him for attention.

The father, increasingly annoyed at having been awakened three times, rose from the sofa and walked through the house in search of the Sunday paper. When he found the paper, he went to his desk and pulled from the drawer a pair of scissors. The father hurriedly thumbed through the paper until he came to the front page of the travel section where he found a large picture of the world. The father took the scissors and cut the picture of the world into about a hundred pieces. Then he sat his son in front of the pieces and told him to put them back together with all the countries in the correct places. He explained that he was going to lie down and take a nap and would be glad to play when the assignment was completed. The little boy set out to put the puzzle together, and the father set out to take what he believed would be a two- or three-hour nap. But he was wrong.

Ten minutes later, the youngster was tugging at his father's shirttail once again. Annoyed, the dad told his son there was no way he could have put the puzzle back together in such a short time. But when the father walked into the other room, he found the completed picture, every piece in the right place. Amazed, he looked down to the little boy and asked him how he had done it so quickly. The boy, with a grin from ear to ear, looked up to his dad and explained, "Well, Dad, there was a picture of a person on the other side. When I got my person put together, the rest of the world looked just fine."

That little boy uttered a great truth. When an individual is together, the rest of the world looks just fine. "Together" is not a place or a plateau; it is a growth process. And that process must be maintained. The greater truth is that when a person continues to grow, the rest of the world looks just fine. But when growth stops and the rest of the world looks anything but fine, that state of together turns into something else. It is called relapse.

Misconceptions about relapse abound, especially when it occurs in the life of an alcoholic, drug addict, gambler, or overeater. In these instances, relapse is often considered failure. Not so for the person with heart disease, who can leave the hospital after by-pass surgery and re-enter months later with a recurrence of severe chest pains and the onset of another heart attack. When that happens, no one points a finger at the hospital, doctor, or patient. No one is blamed for the relapse because it is accepted as a part of coronary heart disease. Most people know that if someone has one heart attack there is a good chance that the person will also have another. The relapse is not viewed as failure but as part of the disease process. Just as relapse is part of the process of heart disease, it can be part of the recovery process of other problems.

Relapse can be verification of the need for *total* recovery. For instance, the drug addict may finally decide that enough time, money, and effort have been wasted on drugs and decide never again to touch another mood-altering chemical. The person then sets out *alone* to conquer the problem and resist the temptation to ever take drugs again. The struggling drug addict will go to great lengths to prove that he or she is recovering. The person may cut off all former drug-abusing friends to prove to parents and friends that there is an honest and sincere change for the better. The person starts to look healthier and act more predictable to the delight of family and friends. But what people start to call a miraculous recovery ends up as only a short-term venture. After struggling to recover alone, the addict takes another pill or injects another needle. If handled appropriately, however, relapse can be a productive event. It can be a verification to the drug addict that *alone* is an unsuccessful way to attempt recovery. Relapse does not have to be a point of failure. It can be a new starting point in the process toward long-term recovery.

When a person latches onto some quick-fix tangent in an effort to recover, the person is actually in the process of relapse, even as the attempt at recovery is maintained. The overeater may fast for days and lose ten pounds, but that is not recovery. Stopping the ingestion of food does not change unhealthy eating habits or eating for emotional gratification. The person is actually in relapse, holding on until the next eating binge occurs. The same fat person may begin an intensive program of exercise to reverse the weight gain. But running or exercising aerobically for two hours a day does not resolve disastrous relationships that spark eating binges in times of conflict. Eventually the obese person realizes that it takes more than to stop eating or to start exercising. The person must be motivated toward *total* recovery. Until that insight occurs, the individual is in relapse, on a collision course toward the next uncontrollable episode. The tangent that prevents long-term and total recovery is part of the relapse phenomenon.

When Reality Does Not Meet with Expectations

When an individual sets out to get over whatever problem has caused pain and discomfort, one element can be used as a predictor for a relapse. That prophetic element is expectation. When a person begins recovery, expectations and reality must be very close together. The problem comes when a large chasm exists between reality and expectation. That chasm exists either due to lack of knowledge of what recovery involves or due to delusional thinking that distorts reality.

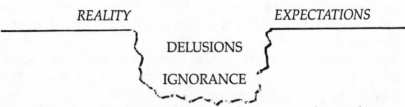

REALITY   *EXPECTATIONS*

DELUSIONS

IGNORANCE

For recovery to be secure, the chasm between reality and expectations must be narrow and void of either ignorance or delusions.

If a person does not know what to expect in the recovery process, relapse is a natural conclusion to futile efforts at recovery. The recovering person must expect that recovery will be difficult and plan to provide adequate protection from relapse. When protection from relapse is not a priority, it is only a matter of time before relapse begins. The person who has spent years obsessed with pornography is going to have a tough battle avoiding contact with sexually arousing material. If that individual thinks that will power alone is going to resolve the conflict or diminish the desire, relapse is guaranteed. Erroneous expectations fed by a starving ego set the trap for a return to the obsession. But someone who realizes that pornography must be avoided at all cost will provide protection to prevent an occurrence of coming face to face with the material. Stores where it is sold will be avoided, friends who talk about it will be avoided, and circumstances where it might be available will be avoided. This self-protection, fueled with realistic expectations about the nature of recovery and relapse, is a vital part of relapse prevention.

The overeater who continues to work in a bakery, the alcoholic who tends bar, and the compulsive gambler who vacations in Reno, all have unrealistic expectations about the nature of recovery and relapse. What each one is doing is providing unhealthy and needless exposure to a situation that increases rather than diminishes the likelihood of a relapse. Often family and friends fall into the same problem of enhancing the likelihood of relapse. Good common sense and accurate expectations will promote recovery and prevent relapse. It is easy to see the problem with a family who serves ice cream for dessert at the first dinner at home for a diabetic who has been in the hospital for three weeks. It does not make good sense. It does not mean that the family should do without ice cream forever, but what it does mean is that it should be avoided for a while, especially during the early phases when the diabetic is adjusting to eating foods without sugar. The same principle should hold true in every family in which a person is in the initial stages of recovery. When everyone works together, relapse can be avoided. Working together begins with everyone developing realistic expectations for the person who has just begun the recovery process.

It must be remembered that short-term results are not the same as long-term recovery. Many actions can produce short-term results—seeing a counselor or starting a new diet, taking up a new hobby or learning to play tennis. In different ways individuals can produce some level of change that looks good to the outside world. But short-term results only serve as a delusion for the individual to convince himself or herself that everything is going to be all right, that things are getting better.

Then when the person relapses, and the person reverts to the old behaviors, everyone wonders what was really going on, on the inside. They question how relapse could have occurred when everything seemed to be going so well. They are quick to find someone to blame for the tragedy. In reality, however, the relapse does not begin with the first drink or eating binge or buying spree or whatever would be termed a catastrophe for the recovering person. The catastrophe is simply the end result of a progression in the total process of relapse. Relapse occurs in four distinct stages: complacency, confusion, compromise, and catastrophe.

The Four Stages of Relapse

The person headed for relapse is on a self-designed path toward catastrophe. The catastrophe, when the person returns to the destructive behavior, will not be a slip or an accident. It will occur because the individual has for some time been involved in the identifiable stages of relapse. When a person is involved in a healthy recovery program, all five areas are being developed—physical, mental, emotional, social, and spiritual. There is evidence of the recovery process because the person is *actively* involved in the struggle to change and develop each area. When the active involvement stops, the relapse process starts. To identify the person who will eat compulsively again, or drink, cheat, lie, or steal is not difficult. The one who returns to unhealthy relationships and once again becomes driven with obsessions and compulsions is the person who stops doing whatever it takes to promote growth and change.

1. Complacency ("I Don't Think I Need to Go to the Meeting")

Relapse begins with *complacency*. The complacency stage of relapse is without involvement in every area. Physically, exercise routines are broken and eventually stop altogether. Eating patterns move from healthy to unhealthy and then into the realm of out-of-control. Mentally, the person stops paying attention to what information goes into the brain. Television once again becomes the main pastime as lectures, tapes, books, and meetings are discontinued. Emotionally, the person stops growing as isolation once again becomes a way of life. Ongoing accountability with a group of concerned others is halted as complacency sets in and attendance at the group stops. The person loses touch with feelings and stops confronting difficult emotions that arise in recovery. Socially, the individual stops going places with people who are a positive influence and a strong support for recovery. The individual returns to the places and people that offer nothing and hasten the relapse process. If social contacts are not negative, they are nonexistent as loneliness and isolation are maintained. Spiritually, the individual no longer searches for truth, wisdom, and meaning. Living a life with purpose is replaced with surviving without direction. With no guiding motivation, the person becomes complacent and smug about life. One by one, those who had been allowed into the person's world are pushed outside of newly erected masks and walls. Although the person not yet participating in the identifiable destructive behavior that was the major source of the problem, it is only a matter of time.

As the person becomes complacent, he or she no longer searches for any kind of guidance or assistance. Humility is replaced with self-dominance and self-reliance. As relapse deepens, the efforts to justify the change toward inaction intensify. The person moves from a humble search for truth into an egotistical routine of self-dominance. He or she shuts down the openness needed for recovery. As everyone is shut out, complacency and isolation produce misery and pain. Once again, the greatest power in the person's life becomes the almighty ego, working only to the almighty self to overcome misery and pain.

The complacency stage of relapse is usually evidenced by lack of support for the individual. As the ego is once again reigning, there is no external support from relationships and people who care. This lack of support allows the relapsing person to continue without any accountability. Because openness has been closed up and relationships closed off, no one is close by to tell the person that he or she is messing up and that it's time to get back on track. When mistakes are made, a chain reaction of destructive behavior is set in motion. When relationships are not maintained, the individual stops the recovery process through inaction.

A painter needed treatment of an alcohol problem. He had spent all of his money, destroyed his health, and sought help only as a last resort. He did quite well in treatment and was able to accept total responsibility for his recovery. When he left treatment, he followed up by attending AA and going to an after-care group at a hospital. He stayed plugged in and maintained his sobriety. He went to work as a graphic artist and did well, making more money than at any other time in his life. Within one year after treatment he had paid off all of his past bills, moved into a new apartment, decorated it with new furniture, and bought himself a new wardrobe. He felt as if he were on top of the world; his life had never been better. His recovery looked secure, but his problems had just begun.

Will Rogers said, "Even if you are on the right track, you will get run over if you just sit there." Well, that is exactly what this man did. He sat there in his new clothes on his new furniture and watched his new television set inside his new apartment. And he sat and sat in a self-justified, egotistical belief that he could conquer the world alone. He stopped going to meetings, stopped seeing other people he had met in the beginning of his recovery, and unplugged from the reality he had maintained during the initial stages of recovery. Lulled by complacency, he had detached himself from his recovery support systems. He thought he could handle alcohol after a year's "proof." So he had one drink that turned into a week-long binge. Within two weeks he had lost his job, apartment, furniture, and almost killed himself. His girl friend found him, dragged him out to his car, drove him to the hospital, and dumped him out on the curb in front.

The whole relapse process began when he moved out of action and into complacency. When anyone stops doing what is working, the person faces inevitable destruction of recovery. When procrastination and immediate gratification take precedence over moving toward growth, recovery can only be short-lived. Loneliness and isolation leave the person detached and withdrawn, ready to latch onto harmful behaviors that devastate the person and the family all over again. It all begins with complacency, and it ends with more precious time wasted out of a potentially productive and fruitful life.

2. Confusion ("I Don't Think the Problem Was Really All That Bad")

When complacency sets in, it breeds the second stage of the relapse process, *confusion*. The complacent person, caught up in negative feelings and behaviors, becomes confused about the reality of recovery and all of life. Confusion moves the relapse process farther along toward the inevitable catastrophe.

The complacent person, cut off from relationships, becomes confused without others to continually reinforce reality. In this confused state, the individual loses a sense of direction toward recovery, and the recovery system falls apart entirely. The individual, who was once confident with the tools needed to produce long-term change, begins to doubt everything. The person questions the need to eat properly for good mental and emotional health. The person lacks trust and constantly questions what he or she has been taught. The person begins to question the validity of being involved in a recovery group. The confused person, trying to keep things together with no foundation of strong relationships, values, or direction, becomes lost among the doubt and insecurity.

The confusion is compounded by denying the severity of the problem. With no one to drop reminders of how bad it used to be, the confused person begins to doubt that the problem was ever really "all that bad." To reinforce the denial, comparison becomes a constant thought pattern. Self-talk is ongoing in some of the following patterns:

"Well, at least I never hit my kids in a fit of rage like Bob did."

"Well, at least I never became as fat as her."

"I might have been obsessed with sex, but I never raped anyone."

"Well, I did only drink beer which is not as bad as drinking the hard stuff."

"Well, at least when I gambled I never lost anyone else's money like he did."

All of this kind of self-talk produces greater denial, and that leaves the person even more confused. With a raging ego trying to justify itself, denial of the problem's intensity is only to be expected. Accompanying the denial of the individual's problems is the denial of the family's problems. Confused, the person denies that there is need for additional help or that somehow the recovery is a bit out of control. If the person is to get back into a healthy state of recovery, someone in the family must intervene. But confusion is contagious and prevents intervention.

As the individual's confusion increases, family and friends become confused also. They do not know initially whether the person is developing some healthy independence or whether relapse is around the corner. The problemed person can be so convincing that family members, just as before recovery was initiated, become confused and begin to question themselves. They even begin to believe that they are the cause of the apparent miserable condition of the person who is supposed to be recovering. Their own confusion leads them to begin roles that are destructive rather than supportive of recovery. They also become trapped in relapse and need someone to intervene and initiate constructive action.

In confusion, brutal honesty is discarded. The focus is shifted from what will be helpful to what "wouldn't hurt." Thoughts like the following ones surface in a confused mind:

ALCOHOLIC: "A little wine wouldn't hurt."
OVEREATER: "One candy bar wouldn't hurt."
GAMBLER: "Just a look at the racing form wouldn't hurt."

These thoughts, born out of confusion, set up the next step in the relapse process.

3. Compromise ("I'll Just Go into the Tavern for a Cola")

A complacent and confused person eventually becomes a *compromising* person on a path toward a guaranteed catastrophe. Without positive, constructive input from relationships with accountability, the confused person becomes stuck trying to prove that everything is under control. But while attempting to show family and friends that all is well, the person gets involved in risky situations that jeopardize the recovery process. The person moves out of behaviors that are productive and initiates behavior patterns no less dangerous than playing with fire. When positive input is cut off, negative thoughts begin to surface. These negative thoughts lead to doubt, confusion, and destructive feelings. The negative thoughts and emotions lead to destructive behavior. Egotistical attempts to prove strength only produce unnecessary moments of weakness.

Needless exposure to risky situations can set off binges of obsessive, compulsive behavior. Compromise can become a lifestyle for the person in relapse. For example, the person who is sexually obsessed must avoid places, people, and circumstances that are guaranteed to rekindle the fires of addictive behavior. A recovering sexual addict, about to enter a house of prostitution, might say that he is entering only to talk and visit and perhaps to receive a kiss. The foolishness of such bizarre behavior is apparent. The person will eventually engage in the behavior for which such places exist.

Others exhibit behavior just as compromising, just as counterproductive to recovery, yet maintain the behavior in a more subtle, less noticeable fashion. The recovering workaholic who starts showing up for work a little earlier, staying a little later, and occasionally going in on a Saturday is not recovering but is easing back into a former pattern through subtle compromise. The bulemic who stops eating regular meals, fasts for a day or two, and begins hiding food is in the compromise state headed for destruction. Recovering from fasting, binge eating, and then purging the food through vomiting, the bulemic who begins creating a stash of food for a binge is no different from the man entering the house of prostitution for a kiss or the alcoholic going into a tavern for a cola. All are compromising in some very risky situations. All are set up for catastrophe.

4. Catastrophe ("Here I Am Again—Right Back Where I Used to Be")

Relapse is the result of a predictable progression from complacency to confusion to compromise to *catastrophe*. As a result, the dreaded event occurs once more.

Once again the drug addict, who has started hanging out with old acquaintances who are users, asks for just one pill or balloon or bag. The addiction process is turned on and the habit returns to its original level of use and drug intake before the person attempted recovery.

Once again, the overweight overeater acquires the ingredients to bake a favorite chocolate cake and devours it within minutes after it is baked. Or the habit of nibbling all day long begins again. Finally the person is left with more fat and less self-esteem than ever before.

The young anorexic begins to skip meals until finally every day has the same routine of self-starvation. Once again the concentration camp physique returns and hospitalization becomes necessary.

The sexual addict returns to the rituals of cruising the streets and bars for strangers who can supply the next thrill and calm the obsessive urges. Once again the person experiences momentary gratification—and intense guilt.

The depressed person, in a final retreat into self-obsessed misery, pulls down the shades and pulls up the covers in an attempt to escape. But the escape is only a trap that shrivels the personality and destroys the heart.

The gambler once again ventures to the city where gambling is legal. The inevitable throw of the dice spins the compulsive gambler back into the obsessions of the big win.

The bulemic gorges on one of many steaks reserved for an eating binge. The binge comes, and the vomiting follows. After remorse and guilt die down, another binge is followed by more vomiting, and again the bulemic retreats in shame.

The workaholic again is torn between family and work. The children hear now as before those disappointing no's to family involvement. Work details capture the person, and the feeling of not enough time overwhelms once more. The abandoned family, hurt and disgusted, looks on helplessly as the career destroys the family.

And once again, the alcoholic who refuses to go to meetings finds relief in old surroundings where he or she is no stranger. The one drink, designed to prove the ability to control the drinking, an hour, a day, or a week later, becomes a drunken binge out of control. The alcoholic who looked so good just days before, appears once again in a real-life drama of Dr. Jekyll and Mr. Hyde.

When the catastrophe recurs, the unknowing stand in amazement. They are shocked at how this incredible event could happen all of a sudden. They ask, "How could someone doing so well have reverted so quickly?" The answer lies in the relapse process that led toward the catastrophe. If the unknowing had understood, perhaps they could have taken action to intervene when complacency was in its initial stages. Or someone could have detected the confusion and stepped in to guide the person back to the truths that ensure recovery. Even during those risky situations where compromise was standard procedure, someone might have been able to stop the relapse process before it reached the point of total devastation.

The relapse process is easy to identify in every stage. And it is only a matter of time until every stage has been experienced and total relapse occurs. Some people compromise for years, tending bar on New Year's Eve or performing some other unnecessary act that feeds the ego. It is only a matter of time until compromise and needless exposure produce the fourth stage of relapse. Often people go through weeks of treatment and discover, upon close examination, that relapse is in process rather than recovery. They isolate themselves, revealing only what is "safe" and never moving toward honesty and openness. Some of these people have every intention of recovering. They want it bad but are unwilling to do whatever it takes to change and recover. They are time bombs set to go off when they can abstain no longer. Abstinence does not produce recovery.

Recovery cannot occur in a vacuum. If a person is not plugged in to other people or lacks reinforcement to prevent reentering the problem behavior, the individual will eventually succumb to the negative internal and external pressures. Without support, relapse is predictable. The only way to prevent it is to hook up and stay hooked up to people. Alone and isolated, a person may have periods of abstinence, but that abstinence does not improve the quality of life. The individual who has six months of abstinence followed by a "slip" and more abstinence is only delaying the long-term recovery that can have a life-changing impact on the person and those close to the person.

My brother Jerry struggled most of his life with his sexual identity. During eight of those years he was an active homosexual. He had turned to the gay life out of feelings of being misplaced in a heterosexual world. He felt that he was different, and he entered into homosexual relationships in a search for acceptance and a place to belong. Initially he thought that he had found what he was looking for. He fit. He belonged. And he was accepted with open arms.

But he came to the realization that he had no satisfaction in living as a homosexual. He needed support and understanding, and he sought out my wife, Sandy, and me to talk about the task of returning to heterosexual relationships. He became desperate to change. He had thought of suicide, had considered it often, but he wanted to make the effort to put his life back together. He had not given up yet.

Jerry, deeply depressed, wanted to change. The principles of recovery could help him to recover and lead the lifestyle that he wanted. But if he did not follow a few simple steps toward change, he would either relapse into the lifestyle he wanted out of or he would finally destroy himself.

He needed to do four things. The first thing was to avoid any relationships with a female for one year. If he had tried to fix the problem by turning to a female, he would have been set up for failure. Change does not occur overnight, and he would need plenty of time to adjust before being capable of an honest and successful relationship.

Second, if he really wanted to change, he would have to cut off contact with friends and acquaintances who were homosexual. That would probably be the major and most painful thing for him to do. If healthy, supportive relationships were to be established, the old relationships would have to be terminated.

Third, he needed to find a counselor in his city to provide him with some intensive psychotherapy. He was not ready to open up in a group, and his problem was so complex that only a skilled therapist would be able to sort out the problems and support the needed changes.

Fourth, he needed to find a church where he could be comfortable and begin to search out some of God's wisdom and guidance through this difficult time. The best thing would be for him to sit back, soak in what was taught, and gradually try to open up to some of the supportive people in the church. He should try to thwart his need to lead and try to belong. In the process, the spiritual problems that he had dealt with for years could be resolved. In all his life, it appeared that he had acknowledged nothing or no one as more powerful or knowledgeable than himself.

After talking about his problem with his friends, he began a recovery program almost opposite from the one that had been suggested. The one thing he did was to attend church. But instead of just becoming a member, he signed up to teach a Sunday school class. He simply could not sit back and be part of something. So he looked good, but his misery persisted.

He also very quickly became involved with a female. She was a beautiful, charming person who cared for him very much. But she could never break through to the real him, and the relationship did not last long.

He didn't separate from his old friends, and he didn't seek out a therapist. So what started out as a lonely struggle toward change ended up as another lonely struggle to survive. Eventually, another man moved into his house with him. He relapsed back into the world he fought to be free of.

Had he really wanted to change? Could he have changed? Or did he want temporary relief from emotional pain? In a moment of desperation and depression, he wanted his life to be different. He was tired of a lifestyle that had proved more painful than what he knew before he entered it. And he wanted out. Because he did not develop a healthy recovery system, relapse back into the lifestyle he wanted out of was inevitable. Because he did not implement a constructive recovery system, he became a victim of his own complacency. His attempt to change was an effort in isolation that never produced desired results. Rather than traveling a road toward growth, change, and recovery, he traveled a path full of confusion and compromise from the beginning.

The story of Jerry's life does not end there. Two years later he made another effort to get out of the gay world. This time he made it out, forever. But he took something with him he had not bargained for. When he left his homosexual friends, he took with him the AIDS virus. Through the struggle, his relationship with God was strengthened. He made peace with his creator, and on June 13, 1988, he died.*

Jerry's relapse cost him his life. The last relapse has cost many others their lives also. With the proper recovery plan, however, such deadly consequences can be avoided.

One final point must be stressed. Relapse is never final. There is always hope for the person in relapse. Recovery can begin again at any point along the relapse progression. For anyone who has attempted recovery only to relapse time and time again, there is always hope. But the individual must plug in to people and stay plugged into them. The power of fellow strugglers working together to support each other in positive change can never be underestimated. Without that support, what appears to most as a slip into relapse is actually a predictable event. But rather than being a point of failure, relapse can be a new beginning. It can be a call to attempt recovery in a different way, a way that produces long-term results rather than temporary change.

---

*Jerry's entire story can be read in the moving book, *How Will I Tell My Mother?*, published by Oliver-Nelson Books.

T H I R T E E N

Hitting Bottom

Snoopy, the wise, modern philosopher, once said, "It doesn't make any difference whether you win or lose—until you lose!" Then it makes a big difference!

What a great observation concerning human nature. For most people, motivation to change and genuine appreciation for life don't occur until they experience loss. The principle is absolute: *only when you come to the end of yourself does life truly begin.*

Coping by Copping Out

So why is it that masses of people on the road to recovery make a sharp turn down the road to relapse? The answer is that they have not truly hit bottom yet. Hitting bottom is when you realize that you cannot do it on your own. It's coming to the end of yourself. Hitting bottom is the most significant step toward recovery.

But hitting bottom is avoided at all cost because of the pain. It's just natural to run from all pain. Sometimes when I ride in an elevator I imagine what I would do if it fell. I would wait until just before the point of impact and jump my best jump into the air in an attempt to break the fall. Now, of course, timing is everything. In a sense, stuck people do the same kind of thing in order to break the falls in life. They scramble as if their lives depended on it. They'll do practically anything to avoid or cushion the fall. But the attempts that protect them from the pain also prevent them from entering genuine recovery.

We have become a society that has learned well how to cope with its problems. Coping is actually a variety of coasting. It's doing anything and everything in order to handle a problem rather than to face it and solve it. Most people feel that if they can avoid the pain now, the problem will somehow disappear in time. But that's not true. Coping is a cop-out. When we avoid the pain today, we are only postponing it to a later date. And later it seems to be more intense and more painful. *Avoid the pain today, face disaster later. Face pain today, avoid disaster later.* Every time we put off the inevitable pain, a balloon payment mounts up for us later.

Coping is the "safe" thing to do with "no risk" attached at the moment. A person is coping when she regularly takes pills for her depression rather than working through and getting to the root of her problem. A lonely woman is coping when she totally immerses herself in her work or children or clubs or athletics instead of facing the pain of confronting her husband's contribution to her problems. A person is coping when he gets busy with work or sports or guys rather than facing the fact that he is not meeting the needs of his family.

The most common coping style is preoccupation. To avoid facing the pain of the various problems of life, a person will drink or abuse drugs or gamble or go from affair to affair looking for anything to take away the pain, even if it's just for the moment. It's a search for anything that will produce temporary, fast pain relief.

Coping is a way of turning off your problems. You can turn off your problems by turning on the TV or radio or tape deck. Coping is also turning off relationships that don't work according to your plans. If you don't like the pain, you can divorce your problems away. That's coping. It's a cop-out.

Coping also occurs by shifting problems. An alcoholic may stop drinking but then start having affair after affair. He or she is still stuck. It's just a different label.

A celebrity drug addict had an emotional religious experience years ago that freed him from his drugs. He became almost fanatic in his new bent—for God. Just a few weeks ago, nearly five years after his religious "freedom," he was arrested for possession of cocaine. What happened? How did he get back into drugs after all that time? The answer is that he never truly recovered; he simply substituted a new addiction in place of his old one. He was dependent on drugs, then he became obsessed with the magic of a religious experience. He was driven in his religious life to experience bigger and better things, but each religious experience served only to help him deny his drugs a little longer. His religious experience lacked a spiritual dimension. He never dealt with his original problems; he only shifted them. He was still dependent with a different label. He was coping.

A similar experience was that of a woman who was dramatically "healed" of her alcoholism. She fanatically sought after every Bible study and healing service she could attend. She gave her testimony of how God had instantaneously healed her from alcoholism. Then the inevitable happened. In the midst of a depression, she reached for the bottle once again. At this time this sweet, well-intentioned woman questioned her spiritual experience, the authenticity of her Bible, and the reality of her God. There is no doubt that instantaneous healings or spontaneous recovery from alcohol and drugs can be documented, but this wasn't one of them. She was coping, using her religious experiences to deny the pain of her real problem. Now she's in a deeper level of relapse and is removing God from her life altogether. Because God didn't make her recovery *easy*, with instant healing, she totally rejected God.

The Bridge Toward Happiness

A continual, almost innate, coping process undergirds every human being. It's the ultimate cop-out. This coping process revolves around what makes a person happy. In other words, what moves you from unhappy to happy? What is the bridge that gets you from one to another? Coping occurs here by operating on the basis of wrong expectations of what will make you happy.

UNHAPPY $\longrightarrow$? $\longrightarrow$ HAPPY

Some individuals operate under the assumption that *people* can make them happy. They try to be associated with the "right" people. Many embark on marriage expecting their mates to make them happy. Disappointment is heavy when these super, terrific people they have chosen to make them happy, make them sad. People cannot make them happy. People may contribute to their happiness or share it with them, but they are on their own when it comes to being happy.

Others cope by expecting *places* to make them happy. I live in one of the most beautiful places on earth—Newport Beach, California. We don't have the woes of Los Angeles, the winters of Siberia, or the poverty of Calcutta. Newport Beach, positioned on the Pacific Ocean, is almost a fantasy world. It's hard to believe that any place could be so clean, so beautiful, so perfect. There are only seven places in all of the world where the ocean air and desert air meet, and Newport Beach is one of them, with a moderate climate of forty-eight degrees to seventy-eight degrees year-round. But in the midst of this earthly paradise, there is trouble, mega-trouble. People who live in $6 million or $7 million homes are just as happy or unhappy as people who live in less expensive homes. Places don't make you happy.

Still others cope by expecting *things* to make them happy. When such people are in a depression, there's nothing like a good shopping spree or even just one big purchase. A young man had lots of toys. He had three yachts—one in the Mediterranean, one in the Pacific, and one in the Atlantic. He owned four homes—a desert home, an ocean-front estate, a mountain hide-away, and a chalet in Switzerland. He was also into cars, both classic and new. He had thirty-seven! But he told an acquaintance, "I'm miserable. I'm simply not happy." Things cannot make people happy. A T-shirt expresses this line of thinking: "The man who dies with the most toys wins!"

UNHAPPY $\longrightarrow$? $\longrightarrow$ HAPPY

People

Places

Things

People, places, and things cannot make you happy. You are responsible for that by learning to re-enter life's processes of becoming (choosing), relating (caring), and achieving (creating). It's like taking a bath—nobody else can do it for you.

Coping takes you down the path toward relapse. Relapse is inevitable when you shift into coping rather than confronting your problems head-on. Coping is a noble try to avoid the pain of life, but by avoiding the pain you also avoid the process of recovery. Coping protects you from pain but keeps you from the most significant step toward recovery, *hitting bottom*.

It's Not a Question of If, but When

On the way to hitting bottom, people grab hold of any way possible to delay the inevitable. If you are stuck, you will hit bottom. It's an absolute. It's not if, but when. There are four possible ways to bottom out. Only when you hit bottom are you able to come to the end of yourself and re-enter the processes of life.

1. Hitting Bottom Through Losing Everything

The first way a person hits bottom is by losing everything. Because of a problem, a person may suffer the loss of marriage, family, friends, business, health, and home. Nothing is more pitiful than this. Life is all over. There is no turnaround without making dramatic changes with respect to the problem. This person is in a back-against-the-wall position. It's choose either life or death, recovery or ruin. Obviously, this is not the most desirable way to bottom out.

Skid row is full of people who have lost everything. Any of those people could get up and get off skid row and recover. But once everything is lost, motivation to change is also lost. When all is lost, the chance for recovery is diminished greatly.

2. Hitting Bottom Through Tragedy

A second way a person hits bottom is to experience tragedy, a crisis with real wake-up value. It's amazing how clearly people think when in intensive care. The flat-on-your-back position seems to shock people into doing something about their problems.

Some people need a greater tragedy than others in order to wake them up. Harry experienced an abundance of tragedies, but events that would shake most people to the bottom seemed not to faze him at all. His wife left him for another man. One of his daughters overdosed on drugs. Another was killed in a horrible auto crash. His business crashed, too. He lost his house and his car, and his new girl friend brushed death for nearly three months as she struggled with a rare disease. Most anybody would have hit bottom through almost any combination of these tragedies. But not Harry. He seemed to bounce back for more.

Last summer, Harry was in the hospital. He was a very sick man, and he sensed his death was all too near. This time something was different. His attitude was completely devoid of conceit and self assurance. Harry was ready to make some drastic changes. The doctors had urged him to make the same changes many times before, but this time he meant to follow through. Harry finally had hit bottom.

3. Hitting Bottom Through Intervention

The third way a person can hit bottom is through the persuasive help of concerned people. Family, friends, and business associates gather together for a surprise meeting with the stuckee to lovingly and firmly urge the person into recovery. Each person present expresses care and concern for the stuck person. Each one relates events and the consequences of the events that verify the existence of the problem. Participants also express their desire for the stuck person to obtain help. The impact of this type of intervention usually motivates the person to seek help. It is by far the most effective tool in breaking through delusional thinking and denial. If performed properly, intervention can be the most powerful tool in motivating stuck people into starting over.

For example, to help an alcoholic father, his wife, three children, minister, personnel director from work, and counselor met in this way with the man. They all expressed care, concern, and their desire for him to get help. They were all loving, but firm. One by one, each person related the events witnessed where his drinking had produced negative consequences. When everyone had finished, the father was asked if he was willing to get help for his drinking problem. He said he wanted to think about it.

Those gathered there continued with the planned intervention. They then presented the consequences of a decision to think about it rather than to do something about it. The wife stated that she would take the children and go live with her mother. The children told their father they were going with their mother. The personnel director stated that if help was not sought, any further problem at work would result in immediate termination. In an intervention, these alternatives for the family and participants usually don't have to be presented, but this time it was a necessity. The alcoholic father entered treatment that evening.

When people intervene by using the entire relational network of a stuck person, it is powerfully effective. It actually recipitates a crisis in a controlled environment. The precipitated crisis usually leads to recovery rather than disaster. Many interventions have helped the dependent person start over.

4. Hitting Bottom Through Personal Decision

This is by far the most preferable way of all to hit bottom. You do not need to lose everything. You do not have to go through a devastating tragedy. And you do not have to wait for family and friends to intervene. You can hit bottom all by yourself through personal decision. You can decide to hit bottom and move toward recovery. "I know I'm stuck. I want to start over!" Through that decision, anyone, no matter how deeply dependent or codependent, can make a turnaround.

Decisions alone don't move you into recovery, however. There must be follow-through. A decision is so easily aborted by all talk and no action. For example, if five birds are sitting on a log, and four of them decide to fly away, how many birds are sitting on the log? The answer is five. Just because you *decide* to fly away doesn't mean you will. Every decision must be accompanied by doing. This is especially true when you decide you've hit bottom rather than wait for the final impact.

When You Come to the End, You're Only Beginning

Hitting bottom is absolutely necessary for genuine recovery. Without it you are just kidding yourself, and relapse is inevitable. *Only when you come to the end of yourself can life truly begin.*

Four men were flying in a small airplane—a priest, a computer executive, a scout, and the pilot. They were only making a short hop, but the plane suddenly lost power and started going down. The pilot turned to his passengers and said, "There are only three parachutes, so somebody must go down with the plane. I have a young family. If I were to be killed, they would really miss me." He quickly grabbed one of the parachutes and jumped.

The computer executive said, "Many people believe that I am the smartest man in all the world. If I were to go down with this plane, the world would suffer a great loss. I'm taking a parachute, too," he said as he grabbed for one and jumped.

The priest immediately turned to the scout and said, "Son, I'm old and ready to meet my Maker. You are young and have a whole life before you. So you take the last parachute and jump." And the priest began to sob.

The scout replied, "Calm down, Father, the smartest man in all the world just grabbed my knapsack and jumped out of the airplane!"

Too many "smart" people in our world are heading for certain death. And all they are carrying is a knapsack! If you are on a predictable progression toward destruction, you *will hit bottom.* But unlike the man with the knapsack, you will have a choice when you will land. What is it going to be? Losing everything? Tragedy? Intervention? Why not make it a personal decision? It makes for a much softer landing for you and those who care about you.

F O U R T E E N

Repossess Your Life

Commitment is vital to a fulfilled lifestyle. It is a missing link for those who have become addicted or have developed a co-dependent life. After counseling hundreds of people and families, I have found that the companion problem to commitment is control. People are out of control. And unless people are in control of their lives, it's virtually impossible for them to make a healthy commitment. *You simply cannot commit what you cannot control.*

Stuck people put off taking control of their lives, and commitments, therefore, are either faulty or nonexistent. It's like the two university students who flipped a coin. One of them said, "Heads we go get a malt. Tails we go to the movies. And if it stands on its edge, we'll study." If you wait for your coin to land on its edge, you'll never take control of your life.

From Stuck to Starting Over

Let' briefly review how going from stuck to starting over works. People get stuck in all kinds of areas—food, alcohol, lies, drugs, divorce, and so on. In the process family members become codependent. The codependent family album is in balance, but each family member is out of joint in an attempt to compensate for family problems. A predictable progression of disasters occurs in a debilitating downward cycle.

The only way addicted and codependent people are able to

start over is to hit bottom. This is the point where they are willing to do whatever it takes. Only at this junction can recovery—physical, mental, spiritual, psychological, and social—begin. The recovery process brings about renewed hope for a productive, healthy life.

That's a quick overview of how it works, from being stuck in a dying cycle to becoming hooked on life. Now let's move through a step-by-step application. In a sense, it's like repossessing your life. There are three major phases.

Phase One: Recognize Areas of Bankruptcy

Personal Inventory: Take a Look at Yourself

Take the time for an inventory of your personal life. *What are you becoming?* Weaknesses? Strengths? *What are your relationships?* Healthy relationships? Intimate? Superficial? *What are you achieving?* Are you making a significant mark on your world?

In what areas are you stuck? List them. We are all stuck, and this is a fact. What are your areas of bankruptcy? How much more pain are you willing to endure before you decide to start over? How much more discomfort? How much more sorrow? Can you admit that you are stuck?

A man entered a psychiatrist's office. He had a slice of bacon draped over one ear, a slice of ham over the other ear, a pancake balanced on top of his head, and a spatula in his hand. He asked, "I need to make an appointment." The receptionist answered with a question, "For you?" "No," the strange man replied. "It's for my brother!" Now, this man had a real problem! Anyone could have figured that out, but the man was not willing to recognize it himself.

Relational Inventory: Check Out Your Crowd

As you evaluate your relationships, you must answer two critical questions. First, is someone keeping you stuck? Who is keeping you fat? Drunk? Drugged? Identify the person or persons enabling your dependency. Realize what they are doing to you. Don't allow them to contribute to your destruction any longer.

Second, are you keeping someone stuck? Are you keeping someone fat? Drunk? Drugged? Do you find yourself bailing people out of their troubles? If so, then you are an enabler and codependent. You are making a major contribution to someone's destruction. Stop being *responsible for* other people and begin being *responsible to* them. If you don't, you end up promoting irresponsibility, and irresponsibility prevents recovery, allowing disaster after disaster.

In order to repossess your life, you must first recognize your areas of bankruptcy, personally and relationally! You must admit that you have a problem.

Phase Two: Reappoint Yourself Executive Director

Take control of your life. Reappoint yourself executive director of your own life. That's right, you call the shots concerning your life. You initiate making personal choices. You initiate caring for others. You start making things happen rather than waiting for things to happen.

Don't wait. Take charge *now*. Take full responsibility for your life. For wise decisions, you get the credit, the prize. For foolish decisions, you get the blame, the price must be paid. It's time to start the things that promote life and living.

But it's also time to stop the things that promote death and dying. It's time to STOP.

1. STOP making promises.
2. STOP holding on to false hopes.
3. STOP hanging out with people worse off than you.
4. STOP calling crisis hot lines and spending hours only talking about the problems.
5. STOP complaining.
6. STOP going from person to person.
7. STOP listening to what you want to hear.
8. STOP talking to people who don't know what they are talking about.
9. STOP procrastinating.
10. STOP exaggerating about everything in an attempt to overcome the emptiness you feel inside.

11. STOP hoping it will get better magically.
12. STOP the denial.

Reappoint yourself executive director of your life. It's time to start living and to stop dying.

Phase Three: Reconnect Your Relationships

I conduct my life by a simple yet profound principle. It may be the most important principle in the *Hooked on Life* concept. Remember this principle, never forget it: *Everything works best when it's plugged in!*

Reconnect your relationships. In order to repossess your life you must reconnect yourself with God and with healthy relationships. Three steps will plug you in and sum up all three phases of repossessing your life. These are the steps that lead directly to genuine recovery. This is not a shortcut, but it's the shortest distance between stuck and starting over. With these three steps you'll be well on your way to being hooked, Hooked on Life!

Step No. 1: "I Can't"

Talk to someone who is experienced with your particular problem or is a professional in the field. Counselors, psychologists, psychiatrists, ministers, and self-help groups are all available to help you get hooked on life. It's a scary thing to place your trust in a stranger, and it is difficult to know who to call for help. It's hard to know the training and ability of the people-helpers in your community. "Can they really help me?" is a common question. If you cannot determine the one or ones to call for help, then call us at *1-800-4-HOOKED*. We have a network of people-helpers all over the world who will help you through any area of stuckness. If you are willing to do whatever it takes and admit you can't do it alone, you can find help.

Step No. 2: "God Can"

A young boy believes in Santa Claus. As he grows older, he doesn't believe in Santa Claus. But when he gets a little older, he believes he *is* Santa. That's exactly what most people do with God. First, they believe in God. Then, they don't believe. And finally, they believe they are God!

Most people find God by the process of elimination because *nothing else works.* If you are not quite ready for plugging in to God, at least begin your search. Search to see if God has revealed Himself to humankind. Try God out! I've observed a fascinating principle: Go positive on God, and He'll go positive on you. All those who have tried everything else and now desperately admit they can't make life work alone will confess to discovering God at their point of need. I'm not suggesting a blind leap in the dark, but a rational search for the God of the universe. As long as you keep your feet on earth as you search God out, you can only be helped.

Step No. 3: "I'll Let Him"

As you plug in to God, you'll find that you also have plugged in to yourself. A strong relationship with God enables you to be a more healthy you. Anything short of that is an unhealthy or imbalanced relationship with God. It basically works like this: *You do the possible by faith that God will do the impossible. You cannot do what God can do, and God will not do what you can do.*

Don't wait! Move into action, and get Hooked on Life.

Years ago, a woman was committed to an asylum for the insane. About three months after she was admitted, she made an unusual request. She asked for a larger room, a large canvas, and lots of paint. Every request was fulfilled.

Six months later, she invited the administrative and nursing staff into her room for the unveiling of her "life's work." After everyone was seated, she dramatically pulled back the sheet that covered her masterpiece. What a shock! The canvas was all white—not one paint stroke on it. Everyone politely sat there "admiring" the painting until finally the chief administrator spoke up. He asked, "What is it? Tell us about your painting."

The woman responded enthusiastically, "It's the children of Israel crossing the Red Sea."

Everyone sat there puzzled, but still acting as if they completely understood. The chief administrator then asked, "Where's the Red Sea?"

She quickly replied, "It has parted. Half is on one side of the canvas and half is on the other side."

"Well, where are the children of Israel?"

The woman said, "Oh, they have already gone through."

"So where is the Egyptian Army?" he asked.

"Oh, they haven't arrived yet."

What a shame it would be to have lived your life without making a mark on your canvas.

Isn't it time you got up out of addiction and dependency?

Isn't it time you moved out of your codependent role?

Isn't it time you started over?

Isn't it time you got *Hooked on Life?*

F I F T E E N

Postscript
on Starting Over

So everyone gets stuck and everyone can enter the great processes of starting over. Here are the stories of some who did.

Some People Who Started Over

University Student: Gets Second Chance at Life

"I hit bottom when I tried to end my life in my car. Fortunately, I had a second chance at life. I was able to walk into the hospital on my own, and the doctor said I would survive without any lasting problems. Flat on my back I looked up and saw my dad. It was so good to have him there with me. He stood there crying, and that was the first time that I really felt that he cared about me. That night I told him I really wanted to try as hard as I could to live a more normal life without being dependent on drugs and alcohol. My father arranged for me to enter a care unit to treat my alcohol and drug problems. While I was there I was helped, and so were the others in my family.

"Now the entire family is in recovery. There has been a giant difference in that we are all able to show our affection, our love, and our trust we have for each other. There is a great sense of unity in our family now. Anytime there is a problem, the whole family joins together to encourage the one with the problem to get through it without drugs or alcohol. It is so good to know

that my family cares for me and respects and trusts me enough to support me and my endeavors."
Starting Over.

Business Executive: Applies Personal Management

"My road to recovery started with realizing that I was stuck. I knew I had a problem. Admitting it was important because I got used to sloughing off the problem. The problem had been mine for forty-seven years without solving it. The second most important step for me was to seek counseling and develop a road map. Through the counseling, I was urged to join a growth group, where I found tremendous support from my peers. Today, two years later, the growth group is one of the most important parts of my week. I love it! I feel like I am helping the other guys, and I know they are helping me.

"Most of my life I have been stuck in business. But now I want to be hooked on life!"
Starting Over.

"Teen-Age" Woman: Learns to Live, Love, and Trust

"I was able to start on the road to recovery when I heard about a support group. I got involved with them and was able to stay clean, sober, and really became sort of hooked on people. It was the first time in my life I have ever been able to take advice from anyone and actually start trusting people.

"It is not something that happens overnight. The first seven months of cleaning up and getting sober I felt very sick. I went through periodic withdrawal symptoms all over again, repeatedly. I still was not trusting that many people, but bit by bit I was able to relate to my group of people who understood me. For years, I had seen psychologists and psychiatrists, but I just could not hear what they were saying. I always felt worse after my appointment. I knew I had problems, but I would not receive their help. Then I met people in this group who understood, because they also were going through the same kinds of things. I trusted them and found a new respect for people.

"In addition to trusting, I am finally getting back a conscience. I had abused my conscience for so long that I had no idea what was right or wrong.

"I think the key for me staying in the recovery process is to never forget where I came from—how bad things were, how desperate I felt, and how I was obsessed with killing myself. Even in the first few months of my recovery, I was not sure if I was going to live. But right in the midst of this struggle, I came to realize that it does not matter how I got into my mess. The steps for starting over are the same. It is reaching out, taking hold of someone's hand, and starting to learn to live, love, and trust again.

"I used to be hooked on drugs, alcohol, men, and parties, but now I am getting hooked on life!"
Starting Over.

Songwriter: Stops Trying to Be God

"On the road to recovery I realized that I had been playing God and yet I was in need of God myself. I desperately wanted to control, and yet I was out of control. I realized that I could not live life on my own any longer, and I made a conscious, logical decision to turn my life over to God.

"Amazing things began to happen. I started relating to people. I related to my wife that I had problems. Before this I was unable to admit to anyone that I was wrong. I remember standing in front of this group of very supportive friends and saying, 'I am a workaholic and I am an agoraphobic.' Now, I let God be God. That frees me up to be me. I have been in recovery for over seven years and have enjoyed positive changes in me, my family, and my music. I was hooked on a lot of things, including drugs, but now I am hooked on life!"
Starting Over.

Another University Student: Finds New Purpose

"Through helpful relationships I have been able to get free from the grip of alcohol and drugs. I love my family, and I

216

know for the first time that my mom and dad really love me. I have a new purpose for living now. My life is not just a boring existence. It is filled with meaning and fullness."
Starting Over.

Nurse: Discovers Self-Worth

"The key to my starting over was being open, to tell people what happened to me and to let them help me. I just did not know enough about my problem to help myself. Now, I have had lots of therapy and have joined several recovery programs. Through these sources of help, I have gained the strength to confront my parents. I have had to tell my mother thirty years later about what happened to me when I was a little girl. I have had to confront my dad and tell him what he did to me was a very bad thing. It was wrong to molest me.

"A very important part of my recovery was realizing that it was not my fault. I did not need to be ashamed any more. I had always felt ashamed. I had always felt different from everybody else all of my life. I thought I was a dirty person. I felt damaged and ugly, like I was not myself. He did that to me, so I need not feel ashamed today. I have value. I have worth. I am OK! I believe today that God loves me just the way I am.

"My life today has a lot of good things in it. Today I am not suicidal. I am not depressed. It is such a gift to wake up and not feel depressed. And I have good, healthy relationships with people. I am able to love people and allow them to love me. I can hug people now and tell them I love them. Another thing I could never do before was ask for help. I never thought I was worthwhile enough to do so.

"I have been hooked on lots of things in the past. I was hooked on drugs and alcohol and food and sick relationships, and now today I am hooked on life!"
Starting Over.

Homemaker: Loses Two Hundred Pounds

"Starting over for me happened when I asked a friend for help. I had a need for someone to love me with tough love—to

be on my team and yet to hold me accountable to my commitments, to understand my problem but at the same time confront me when I leaned toward relapse into my old patterns. In my case, I felt I knew what to do, but I needed someone who cared enough to help me do it. Now, nearly two hundred pounds lighter over the last three years, I am not a blob anymore. I am a real live person. Now I have thrown away all of the huge clothes along with all of my worthless diets and excuses. I have decided to get hooked on life!"
Starting Over.

Secretary: Focuses on Life

"It hasn't been easy to recover from my great loss. But other people who understand what it means to lose a child have given me great support. I have been able to pick up the pieces of my life and start over again. I'm not only progressing in my recovery process now, but I am also involved in helping others who are having similar experiences. At my lowest moments I used to feel worthless. Now I know that I am a valuable person. There's no other way to live. I am truly becoming hooked on life!"
Starting Over.

Cheerleader: Offers Hope for the Physically Challenged

"I realized my handicap was not in losing my leg. My real handicap was in my head. It was my faulty thinking that had me stuck. Now I see myself as productive and growing. I'm married today and have two beautiful children. I'm not living a normal life—I'm living a super-normal life. I'm involved with people who are stuck where I was and I can offer hope for the physically challenged. Yes, I'm hooked. I'm hooked on life!"
Starting Over.

From Stuck to Starting Over.

All are stuck and all can start over. Remember, starting over involves a series of choices and changes and being willing to do whatever it takes. *Hooked on Life* does not demand dramatic or miraculous choices and changes. *Hooked on Life* requires making only one decision at a time and living only one day at a time.

No matter how complex, life is manageable. It can work! People are able to emerge successfully from all varieties of stuckness. But life cannot work in a vacuum. Life is only manageable in partnership with others.

One important caution: *Not all problems are equal in severity. Therefore, not all people recover equally.* For a few, recovery may be immediate. Some may be in the process of starting over for months. Still others may take years to enter into total recovery. It is extremely important not to compare yourself with anyone else's recovery rate. You did not become stuck instantly. Neither will you recover instantly. But you *can* recover.

> As a frog was hopping along, he heard his rabbit friend screaming for help. "Help! Somebody, please help! I am stuck in this hole and I can't get out!" The frog quickly went after a ladder in order to get closer to the rabbit to pull him out of his hole.
>
> The frog exhausted himself dragging the ladder back to the rabbit, only to find the rabbit standing outside the hole. Exasperated, the frog said, "What happened? I thought you were stuck and could not get out of your hole!"
>
> The rabbit responded with, "I was stuck! I could not get out at all! Then a snake came in the other end, and I did!"

You, too, can change "I can't" to "I did." Come along and get *Hooked on Life*, and go from stuck to starting over!

A very wise man said, "I do not fear the ending of my life. I fear that my life will have never begun." Isn't it time to begin your life? Isn't it time to get *Hooked on Life*?

Now that you've read the book, begin the process!
Call
1-800-4-HOOKED
No matter how or where you are stuck,
We'll help you move from stuck to starting over.

- Tired of all the loneliness?
- Are you hating the one you love?
- Do you live with someone who needs help?
- In trying to sleep with someone you respect, did you lose yours?
- Are all of your one-night stands making you feel worse every morning?
- Even though you're in a wheelchair, is your biggest handicap your attitude?
- Are you taking drugs or are drugs taking you?
- Wonder if you're just weak-willed? No weak-willed person has called us yet.
- Gambled away your last dime? This phone call doesn't need one.
- Rather than pick up another drink, pick up the phone.
- If your problem is weight, don't wait.
- When you're at the end of your rope, it's time to talk to the person at the other end of the line.

If you've reached the bottom,
If you feel out of control,
If you don't know where to turn
Call
1-800-4-HOOKED
We'll hook you up with someone who can help.
We'll help you move from stuck to starting over.

We care about *your* tomorrow.

To order the following materials, call

1-800-227-LIFE

or write

Outreach Ministries
Hooked on Life Offers
905 Canyon View
Laguna Beach, CA 92651

HOOKED ON LIFE Study Guide (ISBN 0-8407-9033-3)
Designed to be used with the audio study kit, this easy-to-use work-book makes the "hooked on life" principles relevant to each member of your study group and encourages active participation. Included are reading assignments, questions for further reflection and discussion, outlines of each presentation, and space for recording personal notes.

HOOKED ON LIFE PowerSource™ Cassettes:
Tim Timmons and Stephen Arterburn enthusiastically tell how to move from stuck to starting over in four cassettes recorded live at their seminars.
   Cassette #1—*Three-Dimensional Living* (ISBN 0-8407-9943-8)
   You know what you do, but do you know who you are and where you are going? Find out how most of us get stuck—and why.
   Cassette #2—*Starting Over* (ISBN 0-8407-9944-6)
   The bad news is that you're stuck. But the good news is that *anyone* can get unstuck—and you can too!
   Cassette #3—*Out of Your Rut, and Into Relief* (ISBN 0-8407-9945-4)
   Learn the nuts and bolts of recovery as you find out how to recog-nize and avoid the traps that keep you stuck.
   Cassette #4—*Beginning at the Bottom* (ISBN 0-8407-9946-2)
   Discover when, where, and how you're most likely to relapse—and know what to do to keep your exciting new beginning going. You can do it if you know how to apply the principles!

HOOKED ON LIFE Study Kit—Audio (ISBN 0-8407-9934-1)
Everything you need to start your study group is conveniently pack-aged together—*Hooked on Life* hardcover book, trade paperback study guide, trade paperback leader's guide, and set of four audio cassettes.

PLEASE CONTACT YOUR LOCAL FILM LIBRARY FOR
INFORMATION ABOUT THE *HOOKED ON LIFE* FILM SERIES.

Tim Timmons is a public-speaker-turned-pastor, a mender of broken marriages, a man who shuns what he calls the "trappings" of religion. He is senior pastor of South Coast Community Church in Irvine, California. He founded Maximum Life Communications, Inc., to "counsel, influence, and lead individuals, primarily in the secular community, to know and comprehend ultimate truth." Having received his master's degree in theology from Dallas Theological Seminary, he is presently completing work on his doctorate in psychology. He has written ten books.

Stephen Arterburn received his bachelor's degree from Baylor University and his master's degree from North Texas State University. For the past thirteen years he has been involved in programs designed to motivate people with problems to take responsibility for their own recovery at counseling centers, psychiatric hospitals, and chemical dependency treatment centers. He has authored and coauthored *Growing Up Addicted*, *How Will I Tell My Mother?*, *When Someone You Love Is Someone You Hate*, and *Drug Proof Your Kids*. In addition to his writing and speaking across the country, he is currently president of New Life Treatment Center, Inc. He and his wife, Sandy, live in Laguna Beach, California.